TMS

THE MAJOR SOLUTION
TO
SUPERIOR
CLIENT SERVICE

Major D. Lewis

First Printing, 2014

ISBN-978-0615924496 (The Major Solution LLC)
Published July 2014

Title ID: 4530847

Edited by Shannon Saia
www.selfpublishingdoula.com

Cover by Designs By Letto

Printed in the United States of America

Acknowledgements

I would like to give a special thanks to my wife Beryl, and daughters Alexandria, Melissa, Melinda, and Monique for their unwavering love, support, and respect through the years. That level of support has motivated me to be the best I can be personally and professionally and has kept me determined to leave a legacy they would be proud of. And a thanks to the Crew, my very diverse group of special friends and associates, who have accepted me for who I am both strengths and challenges, and has inspired me to strive for excellence throughout the years through our various positive social events and engagements, Go Crew! Lastly, a special thanks to my Editor and author herself, Shannon Saia, who despite a very demanding schedule, found the time to provide top quality editing for this book and kept me motivated to complete it.

Table of Contents

Preface

*"Ask not what your country can do for you; rather ask what you can do for your country."*John F. Kennedy

The truth is – you don't have to choose.

We are all both clients and service providers. But we don't just trade goods and services for pay. Thoughts, ideas, feelings and energy – positive and negative – are exchanged with everyone we communicate with, every day.

How well we accomplish this exchange, which is observed and measured through our behavior towards each other, determines our success and overall well-being. The quality of our lives is in direct proportion to the quality of our interaction with others. We make our lives better as we make other lives better, because whether we are in our homes, in our communities, on our way to work, or at work, we are all connected.

The Client Base

When I was about 10 years old living in Brooklyn, New York, my parents sent me to visit relatives in Bermuda for the summer. I was so extremely excited and pleased about the trip. I had never flown before, nor left the United States, so I couldn't be happier. While on the beautiful Island of Bermuda with its fresh air, pink sand and turquoise waters, I played with the kids every day all day and was having a ball. One day we were riding bicycles down a very steep and curvy road. And being from the United States I had forgotten that the traffic flowed on the opposite side of the street than in America. This momentary lapse in British culture resulted in a nearly fatal accident that left me pretty bad off for the rest of the summer. All I remember before I lost consciousness was seeing very concerned strangers coming up to me with cloth trying to contain the bleeding. Then I remember a brief period on the operating table and that's it. For a while afterward I couldn't walk and had to eat soup through a straw because my mouth had been wired shut. I could see that everyone around me felt awful and were very hurt and saddened by the whole unfortunate incident. Tragedy had fallen upon my perfect little island visit from heaven.

But after I was released from the hospital and had a chance to think about it, I realized I was still breathing and still on summer vacation on the beautiful Island of Bermuda. I then became too happy to think about anything else. Despite temporarily losing the use of my lips, I would sing and crack jokes and tease the other boys without my lips even moving. One of my cousins even asked his Mom laughingly, "How do we shut this Yankee kid up?" Afterward, everyone began to feel much better about the accident and even about themselves and then it seemed all normal again. Even the Doctors couldn't believe how fast I was healing and were very glad to see it. But in fact *we all were healing together.* Subconsciously, all those people I came in contact with in Bermuda shared a tragic accident that day. Their genuine sympathy, empathy and other discomforts were the outward evidence of the internal pain they felt as they looked upon this badly injured kid from America whose wonderful summer vacation had been tragically ripped from him in an instant.

But even as a kid, I sensed my responsibility to the community to cage the negative feelings of fear, self-pity, and disappointment and to give them what they so desperately needed – my smile and signs of healing. So I felt better, behaved as if it was all good, they all felt better, and then it actually *got better and became all good* because we were all connected to that event and needed each other to get through it. Also I didn't realize it then, but all that singing and laughing aided in my speedy recovery. Now, decades later, I still have several scars to remind me of that summer. And when I look at them in the mirror I have a pleasant memory and feel happy, because I was the only kid on my street that spent that summer in the beautiful tropical island of Bermuda!

That summer taught me a very valuable lesson about choices. I realized that it's not what happens in a situation that defines it, but what you decide to focus on, how you feel, and subsequently how you behave that defines that moment. In other words, there were countless things that went wrong that summer in Bermuda. I was hospitalized from massive head trauma and blood loss. My face was ripped to shreds. My collar bone was broken. I received over 40 stitches in various places of my body. I was in a sweaty, uncomfortable cast. I was in pain. Yet for some reason I chose to focus my entire attention on the fact that I was spending my summer vacation on a beautiful tropical island surrounded by beautiful caring people, instead of being back in the hot, crowded, boring Brooklyn, NY inner city streets.

Emotional Intelligence

The internal conversation that took place within me at such a young age was an amazing demonstration of subconsciously utilizing the natural tools available to all of us such as refocusing, emotion control, behavior management, and both positive intra-communication and intercommunication which has since been termed Emotional Intelligence (EI) [1], also called Emotional Quotient (EQ) as opposed to Intelligent Quotient (IQ). Nowadays many highly successful people in all walks of life skillfully utilize EI as a tool that has proven to be highly effective and beneficial in most situations where people (clients) are present, and has given them a decisive edge over those who lack or are not focused on mastering this skill set.

I also remember my years in school as class clown making my classmates and even teachers laugh as I utilized my EI skill set to lighten the moment. It was an exhilarating feeling that made me forget about the challenges and occasional negative experiences in my life outside of school that came with inner city living. I had an audience (clients) and from my private little stage I chose to perform so for that brief period we all would experience a positive moment together.

One of the benefits of great client service is experiencing the awesome feeling of being face to face with an extremely satisfied client who is smiling ear to

---

[1] In their article "Emotional Intelligence," leading researchers Peter Salovey and John D. Mayer defined emotional intelligence as, "the subset of social intelligence that involves the ability to monitor one's own and others' feelings and emotions, to discriminate among them and to use this information to guide one's thinking and actions" (1990).

ear with happiness and repeatedly thanking you for taking such good care of them and their concerns. And you see the genuine satisfaction of a client whose expectations have been met and even exceeded. And right there a perfect positive moment is shared between the two of you. A great exchange has just occurred, in that you provided them a great service and they provided you a great feeling. The addiction to that perfect positive moment shared between extremely satisfied clients is what separates the superior client service professional from the ever-growing number of people out there that give service a bad name. Once this moment is experienced – I like to describe this shared, positive moment as "The Moment of Truth" – you will seek to do whatever it takes to experience it again.

Becoming a superior client service professional is not just career-changing. It is life changing.

Creating more superior client service professionals – and helping you to experience The Moment of Truth – is the reason I wrote this book.

Introduction

I believe an individual's usefulness is directly linked to their individual happiness. In other words, we work better and produce more positive results when we feel better about ourselves and the world around us. The word *Solution* in the title The Major Solution is not just being defined as the resolution to a problem but also as the right mixture of ingredients that becomes our potion for successful professional and personal life experiences. This book is not just a typical "Client Service Training" instructional guide focusing on different styles and techniques for dealing with clients. It uses the basic processes of many different functioning systems that are common to our daily lives, and some specialized ones, as models to teach and illustrate success by focusing on their individual properties in very effective ways.

It is also a philosophical self-improvement approach that will empower you to develop the skills to focus on the positive aspects of your everyday life and to properly control the negative ones to accomplish your goals and desires. This will enable you to improve your overall client service effectiveness and enhance your personal, professional, family, and community life positively, having a direct influence on your ability to produce quality results in and outside the workplace. In most cases, the people around you will notice the change and respond positively towards you as well. The Major Solution to Superior Client Service asks the question, what really makes us happy? And explains why being happy is so important in producing superior results. The

Major Solution helps you to look inward to discover what happiness really is for *you*.

At some point, corporate America will realize that people can not show up to work and consistently produce their best quality results if they are distracted by so-called "non-work-related" issues. The very distraction makes it work-related, as it is affecting their focus and the quality of their best product while at work! And when we try to compartmentalize our lives, just getting through the day, desperately looking for the end of it so "life" can resume, we miss golden opportunities to seize the moment and continue to live a great life even during working hours. We miss opportunities to make vital, even life-changing connections with potential mentors and partners placed in our paths for our growth and further understanding of us and our purpose. The Major Solution suggests we connect our day as a whole, and keep the at-my-best momentum going throughout the entire day with zest and energy. Believe me, your clients, associates, family, and friends will notice the difference.

This is not some feel-good training that suggests just thinking happy thoughts will make all your problems go away and magically increase your job skills and professional advancement. There is some work involved as you will see in later chapters that will equip you with the proper tools to become a superior client service professional. And unless the client service professionals are actually happy, content in their personal and professional lives, any feel-good training will not last long. And their real-life situations will cause them to become distracted, which affects job performance. It's hard for a sales clerk, with money problems to totally focus on giving exact change all day, and worry about how the clients perceive their friendliness. Or for a mechanic in the midst of a contentious divorce to provide the best service and listen intently to client vehicle problems. Or for a doctor whose daughter has drug problems to sustain the level of bedside manner required to make his patients feel completely comfortable and feel that their problems and concerns are being fully addressed. Feel-good training has left them unprepared to handle any additional stress brought about by personal challenges, or by the average clients and coworkers who have had a bad day and are looking for a place to lash out.

The Superior Client Service model offers an important alternative and begins from a simple premise: Unless service providers are truly happy in their own lives, they can only provide a limited degree of successfully effective service to others. I don't expect employees to just put on a happy face for eight hours, which can only last for so long and fools only some of the people some of the time. The Superior Client Service model addresses the very core of employee unhappiness, which means addressing not just the working environment but the employee's personal life. A great work environment is easier to obtain when one is in touch with, and is clear about, where they are, why they are there, and where they are going in their lives and why. This kind of self-knowledge also allows employees to be totally focused while at work and totally committed to the organization because their personal lives are not a distraction to their professional life and vice versa.

The Major Solution to Superior Client Service is a training methodology that enhances total service effectiveness by using highly effective training tools, and allows everyone to maximize their individual technical skill level while also mastering individual communication skills. Mark Twain said, "To a man with a hammer, everything looks like a nail." It follows that client service professionals are only as effective as the tools we possess and our wisdom and knowledge to utilize them skillfully.

This Book Is For You

If you work alone or if there is just one additional person around you at any part of your day, then this book is for you. If you are a veteran back home trying to reengage your social system, this book is for you. If you have graduated from college or a trade school and are entering the workforce for the first time, not sure what you really want to do with your life but need to make money, this book is for you. If you need cash now and cannot afford to attend college or just choose not to attend college, this book is for you. If you have been working for years and are even close to retirement or retired and wondering what to do with your life and time that will give you a sense of fulfillment and accomplishment, this book is for you.

If you are very intelligent and highly technical and qualified to perform your job but people feel uncomfortable around you, this book is for you. If you don't need to work for a living but are totally bored, then this book is for you. If you have been successful with your individual responsibilities which led to a promotion, and now have to manage a staff of individuals, this book is for you. If you are highly successful at work, making plenty of money but feel a little unfulfilled or struggle with balancing your time and personal/professional priorities, this book is for you. If you are self-employed and trying to boost your sales, this book is for you. If you are unemployed and need that extra edge and motivation to secure the position that you want, this book is for you. If you have read the various self-help books on the market and realize they all share a common thread of ageless principles but you haven't been motivated to apply the techniques to your life and thus haven't changed for the better yet, then this book is for you.

How This Book Is Organized

The tools introduced in this book are designed to be used by you as mental focusing devices to enhance the quality of your behavior and performance.

Each tool has a toolbox symbol next to it and will be explained and accompanied by a brief exercise.

Each exercise has a weight symbol next to it. These exercises can be viewed as the tool's initial programming and is vital to the successful operation and application of the tools and concepts presented.

In Chapter 1 the Moment Of Truth and service provider/client relationships are discussed. This becomes the nucleus of the book's focus.

Chapter 2 defines The Major Solution to Superior Client Service process, client levels and focus of the Superior Client Service Representative.

Chapter 3 shows that the superior client service professional focus is on two very important skills, Communications skills and Technical skills, and demonstrates the proper balance of the two.

In Chapter 4 I discuss happiness and emotion control which can make or break any great moment of truth experience. Our first tool is introduced.

In Chapter 5 happiness, behavior, and behavioral concepts and techniques are examined. Our second tool is introduced.

In Chapter 6 I discuss the importance of a personal mission statement and how to understand your values and goals in order to create your own personal mission statement.

In Chapter 7 we look at the technical side of the scale and how to increase your performance of any job or task you may encounter. Our third tool is introduced.

Chapter 8 we put it all together and place our system in a repeatable routine and discuss how and when to use the tools.

In Chapter 9 I summarize and close with a desire that we take our personal development and client service to the next level.

Part1

Superior Emotional Intelligence

Chapter One

The Moment of Truth, You and Your Client

*"Learn from the past, set vivid, detailed goals for the future, and live in the only moment of time over which you have any control: **now**."*
Denis Waitley

The Moment of Truth basic definition is a term used in business to describe that time when you, as a representative of a business, come in contact with your client face-to-face, telephonically, or electronically. Your job is to ensure your client has a positive experience during this exchange. The goal to strive for is that they are extremely satisfied and thanking you for taking such good care of them and their concerns. The *truth* is in the eye of the beholder and therefore subject to interpretation. At any given moment in your interaction with a client there may be different versions of what is being communicated. Therefore, a positive experience is subject to individual interpretation. But whether positive or negative, a client will always leave with some sort of an impression of the business you are representing.

The Major Solution Balanced Scale Model

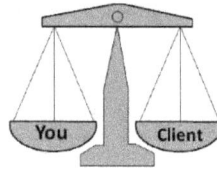

Fig 1.1

Before I go further, I will introduce the Major Solution Scale Model that will be used to demonstrate different focal points of the Major Solution system. The scale represents a *moment of truth* – a service provider/client exchange. Here our scale is an old-fashioned balance model. To use this kind of scale, you place the item whose weight you want to know in one pan, and in the other pan you gradually add small items of known weight until the pans sit evenly balanced. When you add up the known weights in one pan, you now know the weight of the object whose weight was previously unknown.

As it pertains to client service, since we can never predict who or what we will encounter on the other side of the scale, my focus is to make us the consistent reliable known weight on our side of the scale. How do we do this? By first setting aside the "weight" of any previous exchanges or negative conditions we have experienced, and preparing to use our positive, (known) "weights": the tools and concepts of this book, personal development, and self-evaluation.

The "weights" pulling down our client's side of the scale could be anger over a failed product, the pressure of stress, the lingering effects of previous social encounters, health issues or whatever is fueling their negative emotions and subsequently blocking their current satisfaction level. Our goal is to use our (known) "weights" (tools and personal skills) to "lift" our client out a negative moment and up into satisfaction (balance).

You will have noticed that I mentioned we may be burdened by the weight of a previous negative encounter. The Major Solution cannot always prevent a negative encounter. Yes there will be some negative exchanges but not enough to ruin our entire day (and therefore make other, subsequent encounters negative!). I'll use the pixels on our computer screen as an example. The beautifully colored images that we see on our computer and television screens are actually made up of many tiny dots called pixels. The more pixels the screen has the clearer and more defined the picture appears to us. Occasionally a pixel will malfunction and show up as a tiny spot on the screen that is hardly noticeable. This is called a dead pixel. Similarly I seek to populate my day with positive moments of truth like pixels on my daily life computer screen so the more pixilated positive moments of truth I have, the clearer and more beautiful my day appears on my life's big screen. There can be an occasional negative experience the equivalent to a malfunctioning pixel, but that has a minimum effect on the view of my entire great day just as a dead pixel has a minimum effect on the entire computer screen as we still enjoy the beautiful high definition images displayed. Therefore the successful navigation of the positive *moment of truth* is our primary focus and key element we build upon to create The Major Solution to Superior Client Service system.

The Social Exchange Network

"When we try to pick out anything by itself we find that it is bound fast by a thousand invisible cords that cannot be broken, to everything in the universe."
John Muir

Have you ever been in a great mood, and then after just one conversation with someone, suddenly felt like crap? That's because every communication event is a brief connection in a *social exchange network of which we are all a part.* I define that *social exchange network* as interacting individuals that are interdependent components forming an integrated whole. The communication that occurs in this social exchange network is centered on the exchange of emotions and energy, as opposed to intellectual and verbal exchange between defined roles and titles. In the social exchange network everyone is equal.

But not everyone is aware of or focused on this social exchange network, and so not everyone is taking advantage of its benefits.

There are thoughts, ideas, feelings, and positive and negative energy being mutually exchanged with everyone else within your *social exchange network* every moment of every day. An exchange could be something as simple as a passing greeting, a gesture, an acknowledgment that you understand what someone is communicating to you, or a full blown discussion.

I always look for a positive mutual exchange between two people in the *social exchange network.* For my part I seek to give great service and in return I look for the feeling of satisfaction and accomplishment knowing that the client's expectation has been met, that I provided them with a positive experience, and that I receive monetary payment for my time. They don't always have to express their positive experience verbally in order for me to receive my feeling of accomplishment. In this event the monetary payment was given to my primary role as client service representative, and the emotional payment was given to my role as a participant in the *social exchange network.*

The two platforms, *primary role* and *social exchange network,* share the same goal of a positive communication between the two individuals connected to the event. After I realized there are people unknowingly walking around sucking the positive energy out of others I created mental tools to always keep my positive levels high, so despite who I come into contact with, on either platform, I am fully equipped to handle the exchange.

Energy Levels

Just as the sum of 2 positive numbers is always positive, there is definitely a social interaction equation in play as we engage with others. I loosely track it as if on graph paper or in an excel spreadsheet with an X and Y axis to monitor my positivity throughout the day. As with numbers you can have a positive 10 (me) interface with a negative 5 (client, coworker, loved one, etc.) and still be at a positive 5 because $10 - 5 = 5$. So I would still feel okay and well above a negative threshold after the encounter. But my client's experience starting off at a negative 5 (them) interacting with a positive 10 (me) brings them up to a positive 5 because $-5 + 10 = 5$, which is why my clients typically love my services and have great *moments of truth* experiences. Anyone that I've worked with would tell you I appear to be a morning person, hyped up before coffee, but I'm just energized by the network because I bring my positive to each exchange.

Social Exchange Network Benefits

I love dealing with others within the *social exchange network* such as clients, coworkers, family members, friends, and even passing strangers who understand what the value of having positive exchanges with others throughout the day actually brings to their own lives as well. These positive exchanges are totally oblivious to race, age, gender, physical attributes, rank, title, or position. They are not location specific. They transcend all communication devices. So you can be anywhere in the world and have a great exchange from a phone call, text, tweet, email etc. Some of the proven benefits of positive exchanges with others are:

✓ Reduced stress
✓ Better health
✓ Higher productivity
✓ Clearer thinking
✓ Positive attitude
✓ Increased resilience in the face of challenges

The fact that society has not yet focused on or acknowledged the existence of this human *social exchange network* connection makes it no less real. And because many spend much of their time and energy focusing on our differences – swallowed in a pool of negativity, which is producing angry behavior instead of embracing our commonalities – does not diminish the existence of this system that connects us and can charge our batteries like nothing else. It's like denying the existence of sun rays even though we clearly feel the warmth from the sun that is 93 million miles away yet connected to us by its invisible rays. We feel the warmth and coldness from others in the *social exchange network* all the time and are positively and negatively affected by it whether we acknowledge it or not. We can't see the wind yet we do see the trees moved by its presence, as we see people moved emotionally and motivated by others in the system without physical touch or verbal exchange, but simply by their mere presence in the room.

As people begin to understand the benefits and profit from treating everyone they meet as their best client and begin to be treated by others with the same mutual respect, they will be motivated to positively engage the *social exchange network* in order to take advantage of its reciprocal positive properties mentioned above. Then it will become easier to treat others well at work and get paid well for just doing what has become second nature. That is the nature of superior client service and superior living as a whole. Everyone connected to the *social exchange network* is a part of my client base and any assistance, motivation, lessons, wisdom, money, care, concern, respect, or whatever I could ever need to be successful is in that group of individuals in whom I treat very well, at the *moment of truth.*

Chapter Two

Customer/Client Service

*"Not everybody can be famous but everybody can be
great because greatness is determined by service"*
Dr. Martin Luther King Jr.

One day my wife and I picked up some items in a very well-known chain store, and while the cashier bagged my items some people she knew stepped in line behind me. She was very glad to see them and started a conversation with them. From that point I was history. She didn't look my way at all after that, not even to collect my money. She just kept chatting with them while taking my cash. As I grabbed my bag I felt as if I'd been robbed of something, and I vowed not to shop there again anytime soon. We all have negative customer service experiences, yet business owners and management continue to place unqualified, untrained personnel in front of us to represent their business and collect our hard-earned money.

We all have a basic need to be heard and understood. We like to feel good about ourselves and the decisions we make, especially financial ones. And when we are spending our hard-earned money, or money entrusted in our care, we expect to be treated with respect and to feel that our needs and interests are being cared for don't we? As the buyer/client for products or services, we want our positive moment of truth, and never want to be made to feel as if the seller or a seller's representative is doing us a favor, or feel as though we are wasting their time while they take our money because they have more important matters or other people to attend to. Well, if you are working but focusing on personal issues or other distractions instead of focusing on the client in front of you, then that can certainly translate into a very negative feeling for your clients. I always treat clients the way I want to be treated when spending my own money. And I let them know I appreciate their business. Once they experience that perfect positive *moment of truth* where their true expectations and basic needs have been met, they will be drawn to your positive energy like a magnet.

Superior Client Service

Superior client service is having an extremely satisfied client who is smiling ear to ear with happiness thanking you repeatedly for taking such good care of them and their concerns. And the client continues a relationship with the business because of a great product and the positive moment of truth experience they receive.

I have been in the client service related field for more than twenty five years. And during this time I have observed what is at the core of client satisfaction and incorporated that knowledge into my interactions with all my clients.

My EI skill set and addiction to perfect positive moments of truth have proven to be extremely successful for me and those around me for many years. I have even been called Mr. Client Service by many who have seen my techniques in action. Over the course of my career in various industries and capacities, I was called whenever there was a dispute or some other delicate issue to be handled because I had the skill to resolve any and all client-related situations. My advice is to stay committed to providing your clients with the level of service they love and deserve, and they will cherish each time they see you. In fact, you will set the new standard for them regarding client service, and they will henceforth expect such level of service whenever and wherever they spend their time and money.

Superior Client Service Readiness

When I teach my classes, I like to hand a chair to a volunteer to hold with both hands. Then I try to give them another chair while they are holding the first one. They are usually not able to hold both chairs because two chairs are too large and too heavy for the average person to manage. The first chair represents the emotional baggage many of us client service representatives bring to work with us or accumulate throughout the day. The second chair represents the service expectations and needs of the clients coming to us for assistance for which they are gladly willing to pay. Then I ask the question: how can we effectively assist our clients and lighten their burdens – take their chairs – while we are holding on to our own chair, focusing on our own problems, drama, etc.? I see great client service and the need to be in the right frame of mind likened to the airline industry emergency system process where we are instructed to place the oxygen mask over our face first and then assist others with their masks. We obviously can help no one else if we ourselves are passed out from lack of oxygen.

We are our own biggest client. Our first priority should be to be fully satisfied with ourselves by focusing on activities designed to enhance the level and quality of our life and the services that we provide *first*. It is also important to have expectations of oneself, and to have those expectations fully met. Once we have accomplished this, then we can happily engage in the dynamic of product and service exchange with others.

Client Types

I use the term Intra-client to represent us as our biggest and most important client within, in contrast to the external client with whom we are seeking to satisfy and have the positive moment of truth experience. So we will focus on 3 types of clients:

1) **Intra-client** which is you, because you converse with yourself using Intra-communication.
2) Organizational **Internal client**, (co-workers) which are all other people internal to the organization working up and down the process value chain assisting in production, support, or delivery of the product to the external client.
3) **External client**, usually just called the client or customer and the person paying

for the goods and services (product) we are providing.

The Major Solution to Superior Client Service Process

Step one: Recognize and satisfy the Intra-client (you) through Self-development

Self-development is the first step of the process as it relates to your satisfaction and feeling of success by focusing on:

1. Communication skills
2. Happiness
3. Emotion control
4. Behavior management
5. Values management
6. Goal setting and achievement
7. Professional appearance
8. Positive attitude
9. Performance Management
10. Education and training

Each of these areas will be covered in detail in the chapters that follow. For now I will simply say that I believe when we are our best selves we do our best work. Again you are referred to as the Intra-client because you converse with yourself using Intra-communication which is covered in Chapter 3.

Step two: Know the company mission statement

Most successful businesses utilize mission statements to define who they are, what they stand for, their objectives, and what is important to them. The mission statement allows everyone associated with the business to know its core values and goals and serves as a roadmap that allows everyone to move in the same direction in support of what is really important to the company.

The company mission statement connects you with the heart of the business owner regardless of what has or has not been communicated to you through management and coworkers (internal clients). The mission statement is what the owner is trying to communicate to the external client and is sometimes lost in organizational lack of communication, personalities and red tape. Familiarization of this mission statement allows you to represent the business owner with confidence and keeps your focus on that big picture.

Step three: Identify the External Client

The entire business process is centered on the external client (customer) because they are the ones by which the money is generated to operate the business. Your goal is that they always feel important, understood, and good about spending their money – in short, your goal is that they are satisfied.

Step four: Identify the client's need (the Product)

Once you know what the company's overall mission is, and you have identified who your clients are, you must understand what goods and/or service you are actually being asked to provide as stated in your job description. You will have a very difficult time both being satisfied and satisfying others if you do not have a clearly written job description that is understood by you and your management. If this is the case you should request one as soon as possible or record what you believe it to be and ask your management to sign off on it. This will be covered in detail in the Job Performance Self Evaluation section in chapter 7.

Step five: Identify the business process of the product being delivered

When I speak of business process I'm referring to the high level view of the sequence of activities or tasks performed to get the product to the client. For instance say you are hungry with a craving for a nice hamburger and decide to go to a drive-through restaurant. We've identified the product (hamburger), and we've identified the external client (you). The high level process of getting that burger to you probably looks like this on a flow chart:

1. You order the burger at station 1 outside and the cashier takes your order, tells you the price and passes it on to the Cook.
2. You drive to window 1 and pay Cashier for your burger.
3. Cook prepares your burger and places it on the shelf.
4. The last person in the process collects your burger from the shelf and hands it to you at window 2.

Step six: Identify the internal client(s) and their role in the business process

The employees *internal to the organization* who depend upon each other to provide products or services that are delivered to the external client are called internal clients or internal service providers. In the example above the Cook depends upon the Cashier to give him the correct order received from us. And the person at window 2 depends upon the Cook to prepare the correct food and place it on the shelf; otherwise they deal with us face-to-face if the order is incorrect. And if enough clients angrily demand our money to be returned they all suffer eventually because the business will fail. So a smart organization recognizes the importance of their internal clients and all share in the common goal of a very satisfied external client.

Step seven: Deliver the product successfully

The person at window 2 actually delivers the product to us but they all play a vital role in that process. If this was done correctly and we received the hamburger we ordered, we should be a satisfied external client because we received the product we paid for. However, the quality of the transactions we encountered with station 1 and the windows personnel will determine our overall client satisfaction and thus their client service rating.

> ✓ Were we greeted with a friendly voice eager to take our order, or were we just asked "what do you want?" Or perhaps asked the right words "may I help you?" but with a negative attitude.

- ✓ Then did we feel good about handing our money to a friendly welcoming face at window 1? Or did they snatch our money from our hand, totally ignoring us while taking the next order through the headset, and making us feel as though we're in the way so hurry drive up to window 2?
- ✓ Finally did a friendly person hand our burger to us, a clean professional-looking person we didn't mind handling our food, and then tell us to have a nice day with a smile?

Physically getting the correct burger to us was the technical part of that process, but everything else was the communication aspects of that process and required EQ skill. If we drive off feeling great about eating that burger and plan to return there anytime we feel like a burger, then we experienced a positive *moment of truth* transaction and great client service.

A Matter of Focus

Take a moment and ask yourself why you are doing what you are doing to earn money?

- Are you only doing this job because you need the income or extra income?
- Are you doing it because you like the people you work with?
- Are you doing it for the growth and development?
- Are you doing it because you can utilize your experience and skills and make a difference?
- Are you doing it because you are needed, or it satisfies a need to feel needed or important?

Whatever the reason you are there it is beneficial to always remember why you are doing it and keep that focus. There can be countless other people with countless other agendas around you but keep yours in front of you. If you don't have a driving purpose for being there yet that's fine because it will be covered in later chapters.

One day my niece called me very angry and threatening to curse her manager out and quit her job because of the overwhelming assigned work load without consideration of my niece's time, family situation and known health issues. She just needed me as a sounding board to help sort her thoughts before doing something she would later regret.

After we examined why she was working there; good pay, good location, needed the income, and actually liked the job 80 percent of the time, she decided to have a calm professional conversation with her manager to express her concerns. The point is, not knowing or remembering why you are really doing what you do especially when giving so much of your valuable time and energy toward it in the process can be very distracting, stressful, and extremely counterproductive.

Working with a sense of purpose and clarity will allow you to focus on maximum productivity at whatever you do which will be highly beneficial to you and others around you. You will automatically develop a consistent work ethic that people will notice and you will ultimately be rewarded for your focused efforts.

Superior Client Service Process Example

Background

At times during my professional career I have been placed in situations where I am representing firms that have delivered a less than satisfactory product or service to our clients, and then I would end up receiving the wrath from the not so happy client face-to-face. In one such case, I was working as a Computer Technician for a small government contractor providing computer support for very large federal government agencies.

These contracts were supposed to last five years in length. However, because of the lack of client satisfaction, the government agency (our external client) was replacing the contracting firms after just one year of the five-year contracts, and this had happened four consecutive years so far.

Interestingly enough, they would ask the new incoming contracting firm to hire many of the onsite staff from the old contracting firm that had been working on the government agency's computers. It made sense to me that this request was made to retain the collective historical knowledge and expertise held by those employees. What didn't make sense is the government agency continually replacing the contracting firms after the first year of their five year contracts, even though they kept their employees around for the next contracting firm to hire.

One day after the federal government agency was complaining to the current contracting firm about their onsite Project Manager and requested he be removed

THE MAJOR SOLUTION TO SUPERIOR CLIENT SERVICE

from the contract, the lights finally came on for me and I realized what was happening. The government agency (external client) was reasonably satisfied with the overall product the firm's employees (internal clients) were delivering. They were just very much dissatisfied with the service being received, i.e., the mid and upper-level client management approach of this contracting firm and their three predecessors (company mission statement lost within management and lack of management EI skills).

At this point I saw the opportunity to put my innate and somewhat developed communication skills to the test. So I asked the government agency and my newly acquired employer if I could have the job as onsite Project Manager.

Application

Now this was a 25-million-dollar account. And the pressure was really on me to produce and change what seemed to be an irreversible trend of failure, and there were those who really wanted to see me fail. However, I went back to the youthful lesson learned from my accident while vacationing in Bermuda, and which was later reinforced for me by Steven Covey's book "The Seven Habits of Highly Successful People": it's not your situation that counts, but how you decide to view your situation that really makes the difference. So I decided to only *focus* on the fact that this is my opportunity to prove myself, do a great job, and make considerably more money, and not focus on the fact that the past four Project Managers have failed at satisfying these clients and ended up being removed from the contract at the request of the client. And a great job I did indeed.

My primary *focus* was to understand all the true expectations of the government agency, (my external clients), even those not clearly spelled out in the contract (The Product). Whenever my client spoke I was listening attentively and visibly taking notes. I would then repeat their wishes and concerns back to them to ensure they knew I understood exactly what they were relaying to me. And finally I would follow-up with an email to all stakeholders, with a copy to upper management, confirming all requests and expectations of each and every meeting.

I also maintained healthy open communication with my project staff team (internal clients) to keep them well informed and focused on what was actually required of them daily (product delivery process), which kept my team satisfied, motivated, and working cohesively as a winning team should. I updated the company mission statement and made sure everyone understood it. I then made sure everyone knew our internal and external clients, our office processes, and all the services we provide under that contract.

The client was so pleased that they continued the relationship with that contracting firm and me as their on-site Project Manager until all the contract option years ran out. They even awarded the firm with their federal government's Small Business of the Year Award!

The Major Solution Scale Balance

I am convinced the reason success had eluded my four predecessors and their respective employers is because they failed to strike the right balance in their client service approach. The fact that the government decision makers and managers kept the contractor's staff as they repeatedly changed contractor firms shows they were receiving the level of *technical support* required by their agency

What was missing was the adequate level of *communication support* needed for the government agency. In other words there was no management of all the stakeholders, which is everyone affected by the work being performed, especially the client management decision makers of that government agency who felt they were being taken advantage of for spending twenty five million dollars without the feeling that the product and service had fully met their expectations.

Those contracting firms read the contract requirements and hired people qualified to carry out the individual tasks needed, but failed on the human factor. They failed to give that client the warm and fuzzy feeling clients expect when they are spending their money. And when we are spending our hard earned-money, or money entrusted in our care to acquire products and services, we expect to be treated with respect and feel that our needs and interests are being cared for.

A lot of highly qualified companies and individuals have been dismissed or fired because they lacked one of the two very important skill sets which are Technical skills and Communication skills. These skills are illustrated in figure 2.1 as the Major *Solution*, i.e., proper balanced mixture of the two skill ingredients needed for the effective administering of superior client service and will be discussed in detail in chapter 3, Communication.

The Major Solution Scale Balance

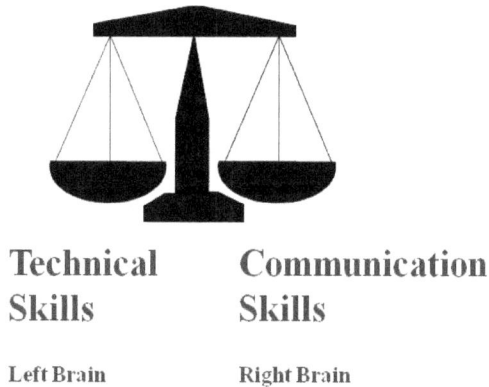

Technical Skills   **Communication Skills**

Left Brain   Right Brain

Fig 2.1

Chapter Three

Communication

Imagine that you are working for a firm that you always wanted to work for and making the income that is allowing you to live your dream lifestyle. Life is good. Then one day you receive a call from your Human Resources (HR) department about a very important matter, but the person who calls you does not reveal any more than this. As you walk toward the HR office, you think about all the possible reasons they might have for asking to see you. You think, "I know I've been on time, well most of the time. I know I'm very proficient at my job, and as a matter of fact, I've trained most of the people here and they come to me for answers all the time. Therefore, I am a vital part of this organization. They must want to give me a promotion or maybe even a monetary award or something."

You walk into the HR office and sit down thinking of how you will spend the additional money from your raise. After some small talk, the HR representative leans forward and says to you, *"Look, you've been here a long time, and you know your job very well. And you are a very valuable part of our organization."* You say to yourself "Yes! I knew it!" But then the HR Rep continues and says *"However, we have to let you go. You're fired. I'm sorry, but my hands are tied on this one. You are a good worker, but we just have too many complaints about you. People say that you are hard to understand when you explain things, too technical, and coworkers and even clients feel uncomfortable around you. And they feel as if you think you're doing them a favor by dealing with them, and that they are wasting your time because you have better things to do. I'm sorry, but we have to let you go."*

How would that make you feel? I hope that this scenario inspires you to ask yourself if any of those complaints in any way resemble you or someone you know. A conversation similar to this one is going on every minute of every business day somewhere in the world, which suggests that there are issues here that need to be resolved. In short, why would an organization get rid of a good employee if the issues that our hypothetical HR person just pointed out can be fixed?

The bottom line is that being good at your job means more than just knowing your stuff. A lot of good people are fired every day because of an imbalance in one of the two very important skills: their ***Technical Skills*** and their ***Communication Skills.*** Each skill-set is very important to ensure successful superior client service, and if you are deficient in either, your ability to deal with clients adequately – and thus your ability to provide superior client service – is compromised.

The Major Solution Scale Balance

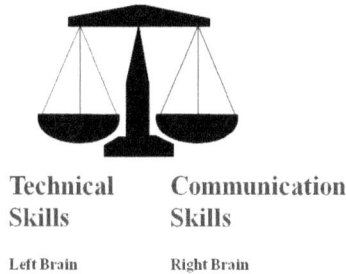

Technical   Communication
Skills   Skills

Left Brain   Right Brain

Fig 3.1

It is said that technical, or analytical, thinking is usually processed in the left side of your brain (IQ), whereas communication skills are usually processed in the right side of your brain (EQ). If you are predominately left-brained, you are probably better at the technical aspects of your job. If you are predominately right-brained, you are probably better with the communication, or "soft/people skills," aspects of your job. The problem with this is that we tend to process information using our dominant side. So if you are predominantly left-brained, you might fit the description in the scenario above. You might be the employee or business owner who explains all aspects of his job in such technical detail that others are intimidated. Or the subject matter expert to whom the subject is so obvious that when trying to speak to someone with less expertise, you always sound just a little annoyed or condescending. Or you may be the person who spends most of the day socializing with clients and coworkers, utilizing your innate communication skills, but who is not very productive, or has to refer to the more technical coworker when the client needs assistance (product) a little above the normal flow of things.

The learning and thinking processes are greatly enhanced when both sides of our brain participate in a balanced manner, and although we tend to prefer one side over the other, that does not mean that we can't be trained to achieve the necessary balance between the two. This is one of the tenets of *The Major Solution to Superior Client Service*: Balanced Thinking = Optimum Effectiveness.

Communication Skills

Unlike technical skill sets to fulfill a given job description, which are usually written out in step-by-step instructions and which will be covered in Chapter 7, communication skill sets are not so easily defined. Interestingly, organizations have not spent a significant amount of time and money in communication training or focusing on actively seeking employees with good communications skills. The lack of focus on the importance of communication skill sets, while expecting communication excellence is a communications problem in itself, and has created difficulties for many people, who have otherwise worked very hard at becoming proficient at their jobs. In fact many people who get promoted to management positions in particular find that they are unprepared to deal with all the challenges that come with that job, which is ninety percent communication.

I am seeing a massive amount of communication skill total incompetence in every part of every industry, every day, everywhere. Just think of the last time you received the kind of service with a smile and conversation that caused you to take a note of how well that transaction occurred and how good you felt about spending your money with a genuinely pleasant person concerned about you and providing you with a wonderful experience. A smile I say? Sometimes we are lucky to get a passing glance as our money is being ripped from our hands, as if to say please move on so I can take care of the next jerk wasting my time. Or have you ever gotten off the phone with a service provider feeling like crap because of the negative energy transferred to you from the service "assistance" person?

A lack of communication skills will always equal a lack of positive exchanges with other people. In fact, it is difficult to be a successful professional if you have negative communication exchanges with others. As a manager, I have counseled many staff members who were very good at the technical side of their jobs because coworkers felt uneasy around them, or because clients would rather work with another person with whom they were more comfortable. You could be the best at what you do in the workplace, but if enough people consistently dislike you, especially the external clients, you are working far beneath your potential for success.

One of the primary truths in *The Major Solution to Superior Client Service* is as follows:

Skillful Communication = Positive Moments of Truth

This axiom is as true in your personal life as it is in your professional life, and therefore, it is in everyone's best interest to pay close attention to the communication process. A person who spends the day flowing through states of positive communication exchanges with others will sleep a lot better than the person who experiences negativity in their communications with those around them, friends and family as well as internal clients and especially external clients!

What is Communication?

Communication is a process whereby information is imparted by a sender (you) to a receiver (them) via some medium. The receiver then decodes the message and gives the sender a feedback.

Read it once again.

There are many variations of this basic definition for communication, but they all should have a message, a sender, a medium, a receiver and feedback at the minimum. As the sender, your messages should always be as positive and supportive as possible. In order for this to happen you need to be aware that communication first occurs within you. This is called Intrapersonal Communication.

Intrapersonal and Interpersonal Communication

During intrapersonal communication you are the sender and the receiver and what you say to yourself really does matter. If your communications skill set is in the early stages of development, you may go through the day totally unaware of the self communication process that is taking place within you. This would mean there are countless messages and ideas being presented to you from other people and situations all day long that you are receiving without them first being filtered through your internal monitoring center.

This can have a very adverse and non-supportive affect on your happiness, total productive output, and effectiveness, both personally and professionally. Consider there is at least one person around us every day that is having a bad day. And even though their negative experience could be valid for them at the time, it is totally unacceptable for us to subscribe to and take on that negativity ourselves. And it is even worse for us not to be aware that we have the option to decide whether to accept the negative ideas and messages, or decide to just acknowledge them without becoming an unsuspecting victim of them.

Self monitoring is not a very difficult task in and of itself. It is remembering to do it and allowing it to become a natural part of your day that is the challenge. The technique for this will be discussed later. Once we (intra-client) have positive and supportive ideas and messages available, we are then ready to impart them to others (internal and external clients).

The process of sending and receiving information between two or more people instead of just communicating within ourselves is called Interpersonal Communication. Some introverts may find this stage of communication a bit challenging until properly mastered. Interpersonal communication gives us the opportunities to share our great day with others and provide superior client service by creating positive exchanges with clients and associates.

Communication Medium

At times my immediate family members seem to know when I'm really upset. And even though I consciously speak positive or supportive words to them, they react from what I'm thinking instead of what I'm attempting to convey verbally. This is because I am sending messages using channels other than just speaking. And they are receiving and encoding these non-verbal messages from the facial expressions, hand gestures, and vocal inflections that I am unconsciously using. Communication mediums are the ways messages are conveyed between sender and receiver both consciously and subconsciously.

Many times body language reflects the inner emotions and motivations rather than the actual intended delivered verbal message. This is why positive and supportive *intrapersonal* communication is so important at the beginning of the communication process, because you can only fool some of the people some of the time. It is very beneficial to practice what you are saying to yourself and what and how you are conveying it to others.

You have probably heard the term "lost in translation"; this happens far too frequently in our everyday exchanges within us and with others.

Because people have different experiences, values, and ways of perceiving, every act of communication includes plenty of opportunity for a person to project a message that will be received in a totally different way than intended. Consequently, it is very important to understand the entire communication process in order to help ensure that the ideas you are trying to convey are received as you want them to be received.

Communication is an ongoing process that includes:

1. How you perceive what's happening both in and around you at any given time
2. How you represent that to yourself
3. How you project that perception to others
4. How those receiving your perception represent that perception to themselves
5. How those receiving your perception represent to you what it is that they think they have understood

I know that was a mouth full, you may want to read that again. In short, communication never stops. It's not only ongoing and dynamic; it's a feedback loop or cycle as shown in figure 3.2.

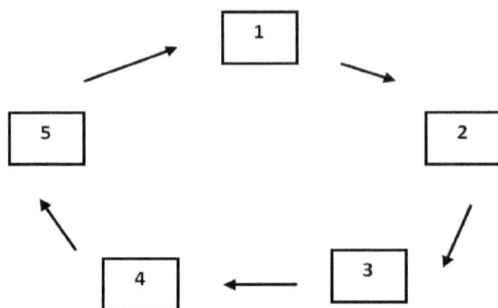

Fig 3.2

This book is the medium I have chosen to impart messages and ideas from me to you. It would probably be more effective if you were sitting in my class at this very moment. You would then see my non verbal or body language, and I could then see your reactions to what you are receiving and utilize that feedback to further clarify and support my messages and ideas.

Understanding how communication affects our lives and becoming skillful with the communication process will certainly give you an advantage over those who don't, and will significantly add to you having great day experiences. Start enjoying better personal and professional relationships that create environments for personal happiness and successful exchanges in and outside your workplace as soon as possible by actively focusing on the communication process, what messages you are sending and receiving, and how they are being transmitted.

Chapter Four

Happiness

A very basic definition of happiness is: a state of well-being characterized by emotions ranging from contentment to intense joy. So that means happiness is an emotional state and not something outside of ourselves that we can possess or obtain. Albeit true that we can use things such as money or vacations etc, to help us trigger the positive and supportive range of emotions that characterize happiness, they are not in themselves the happiness, nor will they always induce it.

There are many different industries and countless jobs out there. And many times we accept jobs because we need the income at the time, or it may be what we truly want to do. Always keep in mind that your self-worth is not dependent on your income or job title. Your job description and salary does not define you as a person, nor should it dictate your state of happiness. Just ask some top executives who are now serving prison sentences for stealing, despite making more money than they would ever need. Their million-dollar bank accounts did not stop their negative destructive emotions and behavior from ruining their lives and the lives of their loved ones.

I know the big house and expensive car triggers a sense of self worth and accomplishment. But at the end of the day, it's how well you do your job and not your job title that should define you as a person. Whether you are an employee or own your business, your self-worth and eventual feeling of contentment and success will be measured against what you do and how you do it, in relation to what you truly value and what's really important to you at the time.

Am I Happy?

EXERCISE

Take a moment and ask yourself the following questions. Then listen for the intrapersonal answers:

1. Am I happy at work?
2. Do I look forward to arriving at work, seeing the people there, and performing my job?
3. Do I even know what my full job description is?
4. Do I hate my job? Or worse – do I hate myself for doing it?

I use to be amazed at the number of people who had never asked themselves what would make them happy personally or professionally, and then waited to hear the answer. The very act of asking yourself the question and answering it is intrapersonal communication.

Self, what job would make me happy getting paid to do it?

I continually counsel people that have spent years in their field totally disliking what they do. Some even retired unfulfilled, are looking for work in which they can make a meaningful contribution, and have still not asked themselves that question or heard the answer. And I know there is the mind-set that I'll do anything just to get paid; then I'll use the money to do the things I really enjoy. And that may work for a while. The problem with this train of thought is that you will never give your absolute best doing something you dislike. Over time, mediocrity will not trigger positive, supportive emotions, nor will it satisfy your need for achievement, and your inner-values will not be satisfied. Then you struggle through stress-filled days praying for the weekends or days off to arrive to rescue you from insanity.

Emotions

So happiness is a state of well-being characterized by a range of emotions. Therefore, we should have control of our emotions and choose those emotions we want to utilize at any given time to support our daily goals and objectives.

This is not as easy as it sounds.

I like the work that Dr. Barbara L. Fredrickson, the author of the book *Positivity*, has done in the field of positive emotions and the tremendous effect that they have on our lives. Her research has shown that positive emotions make us better in every facet of our lives. She has shown that negative emotions like fear close down our minds and hearts, whereas positive emotions literally open our minds and hearts and empower us to face challenges with hope and creativity. She proves that positive emotions are not just nice words to make us smile, but that they change our mindset and biochemistry. Dr. Fredrickson discovered that experiencing positive emotions in a 3-to-1 ratio with negative ones leads people to a tipping point beyond which they naturally become more resilient to adversity and effortlessly achieve what they once could only imagine. With Positivity, we learn to see new possibilities, bounce back from setbacks, connect with others, and become the best version of ourselves.

As discussed in chapter one, connecting with others is what client service is all about.

Embrace the awareness that we are not robots. We are not limited to reacting on impulse and instinct. Instead, we can think independently and then respond rationally to daily events and circumstances. Self realization is what separates mankind from the rest of the earth's inhabitants. Embracing our positive, supportive emotions and controlling our negative, destructive ones will help you to obtain and maintain happiness!

Powerful, positive emotions add to our daily livelihood. How can we remember to access and focus on them throughout our day so we can benefit from them?

The SMART Remote Control

Background

Some years ago I was laying back relaxing in my bedroom watching sports on my television and it was in the last 2 minutes of a basketball game. My team was down by one point and looked to be able to score and take the lead on the very next play. Then out of nowhere my television changed channels. It was a bit spooky but okay, I said to myself, things happen; so I turned back to the game. Then, when there was under a minute left in the game my television changed channels again. I became a little annoyed after the second incidence but waited until the game ended to call my cable service provider to gain some insight and resolution for this issue. The service provider told me the most likely reason for my television changing channels randomly was that my neighbor's remote control was probably controlling my cable box, something that is apparently not uncommon for Infrared (IR) remote controls. These type remote controls were popular because they were easy to program. So the way to prevent this problem from happening was to purchase and use a Radio Frequency (RF) remote control and program it accordingly. Eliminating the IR remotes altogether and replacing them with remotes that operate on different formats was the most full-proof way of reducing IR signal traffic in my home. So I purchased RF remote controls so that I would be the only one controlling my television viewing.

But I got more out of that situation than just control over my television set. I got the perfect analogy for the emotional focus and control tool which is vital to the superior client service representative and to everyone else looking to have successful, positive *moment of truth* interactions, whether those interactions are with clients, or with ourselves.

Application

Visualize a television remote control whose keypad is labeled with different emotions. Using this remote control, we can control our mental/emotional state by pressing exactly which emotions we want to feel. The emotions that we feel affect how we view events. My television was being remotely controlled by signals passing through my home from my neighbor's remote control device. Likewise, we are bombarded with negative signals from others in the social exchange network and from outside circumstances that pass through us all day. These signals affect our moods, productivity, and our ability to communicate internally and with others in positive, beneficial ways.

With the press of a button, the SMART Remote Control will help us focus on controlling our day by deciding how we want to feel and when we want to feel that way. Because if we don't decide how we want our day to go, it will be decided for us by others. And when we are totally overcome with negative emotions, we have the potential to do harm both to ourselves and to others both emotionally, and – in extreme cases – even physically. Consistently regretting or apologizing for our behavior is a sign that we are out of control, and the SMART Remote is a good place to start in regaining control of our lives through the power of positive emotions.

Since our minds are like television screens going from one channel to another throughout our day, not making a conscious effort to control our daily emotions and mental imagery is like allowing our neighbors to control our television through the walls with their remote controls. But once we recognize that there are random feelings and thoughts in our minds that are negatively affecting our mood, and consequent behavior, we can then press our SMART Remote Control button and change the channel of our mind to a more positive and resourceful station, that will assist us to focus on more desired *moments of truth* and productive days.

SMART Remote Control

I Feel		
Awesome	Inspired	Qualified
Brilliant	Jubilant	Radiant
Content	Kind	Successful
Daring	Loving	Tenacious
Exceptional	Motivated	Unique
Faith	Nice	Valuable
Generous	Organized	Wonderful
Healed	Powerful	Zealous

Fig 4.1

SMART Remote Control Programming

As with most applications and devices there is a setup routine required to operate this remote control effectively. And the more familiar you are with it the more beneficial it will be to you.

EXERCISE Setup Routine

Step1: Go to a nice quiet place where you usually relax, like your favorite couch, but leave the television off.

Step 2: Close your eyes and take 3 slow deep breaths to relax and also to give your brain and heart a nice new fresh amount of oxygen to work with. Hold each breath in for about 4 seconds then completely exhale through your mouth.

Step 3: Read the first button out loud while pressing it, close your eyes and think about its meaning, and see if you can feel that emotion as you pass through an imaginary portal. Place the words "I feel" in front of the emotion and feel what happens. This is a very powerful intra-communication exercise between your brain and heart. **Please do not skip over this section.**

Step 4: Experience the emotion for as long as you like. I suggest not using more than three emotions within an hour initially for effective programming. If you have difficulty feeling the emotion you can try again another time or it may show up later on its own. You can also take some time to think about the word's meaning and think of synonyms of the word. You can also use the word as an acronym representing other positive words or phrases, for instance for Awesome you could think of:

A - Awe Inspiring

W - Winner

E - Effervescent

S - Super

O - Outstanding

M - Magnificent

E - Enthusiastic

Take your time. There is no rush. Words are the way we describe and define everything we see, think, feel, and do. Our Positive Emotions are given life and permission to work wonders in our lives through the positive words that define them.

Step 5: Repeat steps 1- 4 for each button. Again, attempt to experience no more than 3 emotions per hour.

Just like your cell phone favorites list, when this setup routine is done properly these emotions will be in your mental favorites list so when you speed dial them they will answer you – their master – and empower you at your command. Remember, as with anything, practice makes perfect, even a committed 5 minute daily routine.

There can also be a positive rush and a general feeling of wellness experienced during this process. Some people drink alcohol or use drugs to feel good, which is actually an indirect attempt at altering their emotional experience. So why not just go directly to the source and then program your positive emotions in your recall memory? At times I spend hours in communion with just one emotion that has me feeling so good or has motivated me to the point I just continue to enjoy its company. And the beautiful thing is that unlike utilizing substances that have possible abuse, negative, addictive, and destructive side effects, feeling great is just that, feeling great!

And as the individual pixels of your television or computer screen make the single complete image we see when viewed, great individual moments of feeling good, make up great entire days one moment at a time, or one social interaction at a time.

So introduce yourself to or re-acquaint yourself with your positive emotions that have been neglected and unemployed or underemployed for so long. And give your negative counterproductive emotions that have been enjoying plenty of overtime employment the boot.

If you want your own hard version remote control to take with you during the day The SMART Remote Control can be ordered from www.servicesuperior.com.

Negative Emotions

I can see the intrinsic value of negative emotions for our primitive ancestors in the times of survival and danger lurking around every tree. Since then, human consciousness has evolved. We have become the dominant species on the planet through self awareness and technology. We have formed complex societies that are maintained through order and structure. We are a lot smarter now, with many more evolved emotions with which to experience our civilized environment.

But no matter how civilized we like to think we are, our negative emotions are still present and are instantly activated when faced with perceived danger. We may perceive a lot of things that aren't physically harmful as 'danger' – like feeling threatened that someone might take our job, or feeling smothered by a parent or a spouse, or feeling trapped raising kids, or trapped in a job we hate. Our old mindset is still operating and we feel those things as anxiety or danger, and express them as fear or anger.

The problem, in my opinion, is that we allow those emotions to run rampant and unsupervised in our daily lives in a peaceful and sophisticated environment where social behavior is so prevalent. An emotion like anger, if left unattended, wreaks havoc on our lives and relationships.

Figure 4.2 is a visual representation of how I view the relationship of positive to negative emotions and their effect on displayed behavior when we are communicating with clients or within our social exchange network (during the *moment of truth*). The negative emotions are down in a subordinate yet supportive location for purposes of control. Yet, as described above, as Dr. Frederickson tells us, positive emotions should outweigh the negative ones, 3 to 1. They are never in the higher levels of consciousness, and should aviod direct contact with the outside world.

I also have before and after *the moment of truth* sections on the bottom left and right to bring attention to the idea that we can't wait until the time of the actual outward behavior display to focus on being in a good mood. This focus should be observed each day as a habit and periodically checked to make sure we have a good balance and that proper housing of the negative emotions is maintained and controlled. And we should keep an eye out for warning signs to alert us if there is a problem and to prevent a negative emotion prison break before it occurs.

Moment of Truth Behavior Display Levels

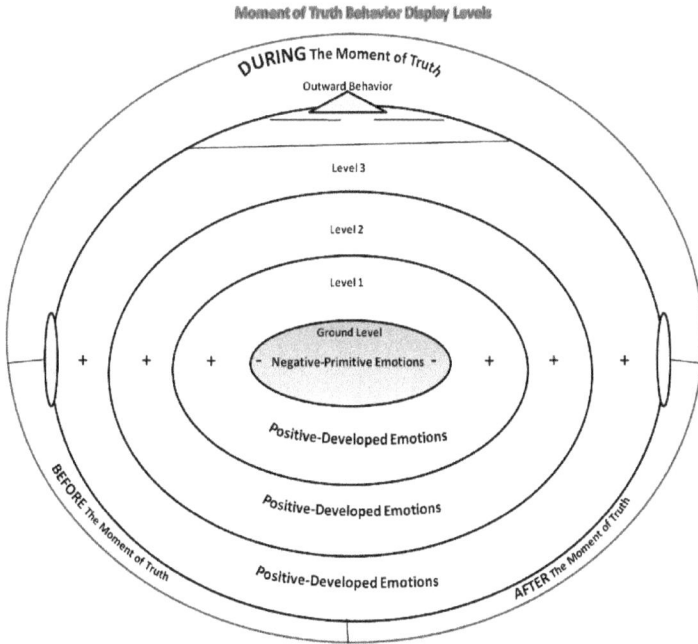

Fig 4.2

Warning Signs of Negative Emotions

I spent the early part of my life living in the Bedford Stuyvesant section of Brooklyn New York AKA (do or die bed-sty). And even though there are plenty of nice brownstone single family style homes in the area, we lived in an apartment building until my parents decided to buy a home in the Bronx. We had our share of pests, to include some roaches, which in my book are at the bottom of the scale of pests. And even though we were pretty clean, didn't leave food out, and sprayed constantly they would always return after a couple of days. That was because in an apartment building unless the entire building is exterminated the pests just went to our neighbors until the insecticide fumes died down then they could return.

One day we went to Coney Island amusement park and I won a goldfish. It was my first pet and I was very excited and named him Freddy. The first thing I did was ask my mom for a small fish bowl so I could give Freddie the fish a home. So on the way home she bought me a fish bowl. I then fed Freddy and said good night.

In the morning when I got out of bed I saw my goldfish laying on its side but still moving a little. At first I thought he was asleep but then I saw the reason for his awkward position in the water. A roach had gotten in my fish bowl and was sitting on top of my goldfish – I guess feeding and staying dry. I didn't even know roaches could swim to have reached Freddy in the first place. I immediately got rid of the roach but Freddie couldn't straighten up after that and my mom told me he wasn't going to make it. So I had to flush him down the toilet which I did reluctantly. I was devastated and have waged war on those filthy pests ever since.

Even today, if I see a bug that even resembles a roach; I go ballistic and won't sleep until I know it wasn't a roach because there's never just one. His buddies are in the wall waiting for the lights to go out. Yes there is a reason I shared this story with you. For me roaches are the lowest pest on the scale and the one I dislike the most. I now associate negative emotions with roaches as the lowest emotions on my social scale

Negative Emotions Alert!

If you ask anyone that knows me they will attest to the fact that I'm hardly ever feeling down or displaying any negative emotions for long. I've turned my dislike for roaches, which I'm going to call Pests, into a way of keeping negative emotions at bay. Negative emotions are to me just like Pests in many ways.

They are the least desired and lowest emotions on the scale of happiness. And if one shows, there are others lurking and waiting to spoil your moment. For instance, if jealousy is on your mind, you better believe anger is not far. When we realize they are present, usually by the distasteful behavior we are displaying, we shine the light on them by using brighter more positive emotions to get us out of the basement feeling. And even when we control the negative emotions they can resurface because when we are around others with negative emotions, they come into our happy space if we aren't careful and ruin our moments, just like that person at work who wants to share how rough the job and life in general is to his neighbors who are just trying to work.

Although I have decided to have great days and have my SMART Remote Control to facilitate that desire, I still occasionally find myself faced with negativity or signs of it and may not have the ideal environment to mentally operate my remote which operates best as a proactive tool. For the rare occasion when an immediate reactive response is needed I incorporated a trigger word that identifies my negative mood before it becomes a problem or noticeable to others.

Emotion Trigger Word

A trigger word is used to initiate an immediate response through word association and can be used in conjunction with the SMART Remote Control. Whenever

I am feeling the presence of negative emotions or displaying behavior which is evidence of them lurking in the walls of my mind, I say out loud, "Roaches!" And those negative emotions usually run for the hills because I'm looking to eradicate their very existence from my personal space. So that word has become a trigger for me to keep me from moving too far into the negative and make the job of my SMART Emotions Remote Control that much easier.

And even if I don't have a preconceived desire to feel a specific positive emotion at the time, it resets my system and places me back on a level playing field without the negativity. So I may not know what positive emotion I want to feel at the time but I definitely know I don't want to feel any negative ones.

Of course, your trigger word doesn't have to be the same. But you should have one for the occasional process of immediate identification and eradication of negative emotions even before using your SMART Remote to choose your next desired mood. Think about what your pet peeve is, the thing that really irks you the most and associate that to the presence of negative emotions and it will serve as the trigger you need to dismiss them immediately. I associate negative emotions with something I really hate in hopes of segregating them from my daily life by feeling bad by their very presence and thus limiting or eliminating their airtime. This places you in a more receptive position to receive your SMART Remote Control signaling or just enjoy the absence of the unwelcomed negative emotion dampening your moment.

Living with Negative Emotions

The only way I see our negative emotions coexisting with successful social interaction is to be filtered through our positive emotions. In this way we get the strengths of them while controlling their reckless, socially destructive weaknesses. For instance, usually by the time my anger is filtered through the layers of positive emotions that I typically enjoy daily and makes its way to the surface the anger is displayed as firmness or strong conviction about something. So instead of it paralyzing my objectivity, I retain all my higher-level peripheral views needed to succeed through social diplomacy in the conversation instead of the primitive display of disrespect or even violence, which tends to happen with unfiltered anger.

And if by chance anger has compromised my desired behavior, which I consider a disaster, an invasion or even a negative emotions prison break, I utilize my trigger word and/or focus on my SMART Remote Control and regain control of myself as quickly as possible by pressing a positive emotion button to change the emotional channel and consequent behavior being displayed.

Those in observance of me feel and respect my strength without any social discomfort or the fear of violence. And as for the negative emotion of fear, by the time it reaches the surface it is displayed as caution and attention to detail, and a strong desire to perform well instead of me being crippled into submission by the thing I was afraid of.

When dealing with the public or anyone outside of ourselves for that matter, behavior is a powerful medium that connects us to that experience good or bad, and is indelible. *"A thousand words will not leave so deep an impression as one deed."* Henrik Ibsen. And our emotions dictate our behavior.

What a client sees and hears from us during the *moment of truth experience* determines their feelings and opinions and will dictate their decisions. And if income is a part of your plan then people spending money around you, feeling good, or just noticing how well you perform your job and telling others is a factor. So as with anything else you are good at in your life, practice makes perfect. Perfect your control by spending more time getting to know your positive emotions and you will reap the social benefits through clients feeling great around you and positive things happening to you as a result of the law of attraction.

Chapter Five

Behavior

"Human behavior flows from three main sources: desire, emotion, and knowledge."
Plato

I would like to think the reason I am not being treated better by client service people in all industries around the world is because they themselves are having bad days or bad lives. But could it be a much simpler diagnosis?

Manners:

"Do unto others as you would have them do unto you."
Holy Bible

A couple weeks ago my wife and I went to a restaurant that recently opened in a new development that we just had to check out. It was a very nice restaurant, a little pricy, but we expected that, and we were very hungry and could hardly wait to order. Our server finally came and we ordered. It took a while for our food to arrive, and when it did my wife was not impressed with her meal. But I was happy with mine, after I ordered an additional side dish to spice things up. My wife however tried to doctor her meal up but was unsuccessful. To make matters worse, our server seemed to disappear for about 20 minutes so I couldn't inform her that my wife's drink was flat as well.

So all in all my meal was fine but my wife was very displeased with her meal and the long wait as she stated to me before our server returned with the check. However after the server left and right before I was figuring her tip my wife commented about how polite the server was and my wife had a smile on her face. I was already satisfied, but to see my wife smiling after complaining about her meal allowed me to give that young lady a decent tip, which I always try to do anyway. That was very interesting to me that our server satisfied my wife at the last moment through one social exchange network encounter which equated to a positive moment of truth and a nice tip despite my wife being totally dissatisfied with the overall product received.

Manners should be a fundamental concept for all of us like potty training, but I have found the basic utilization of manners to be lacking in people at work in all fields and all ages. And it may be my imagination, but it seems to become even more apparent in the younger generations. If you are a parent or plan on being a parent you have an obligation to the social exchange network to teach your children manners, and if you are in the workforce no matter what your age and have not received this training, forgotten, or perhaps just chose not to use this very important social behavior skill set, then please correct this inexcusable flaw immediately. Like it or not, you are a member of the social exchange network, and you are damaging your own chances of success if you are not using manners as a part of your basic communications exchange. Many times you will receive rude or seemingly unfair treatment from others, awkward moments, or maintain shallow relationships, as a penalty for breaking the social exchange network standards of conduct law, *manners*. Common phrases to use daily are:

1. Hello
2. May I help you
3. Please
4. Excuse me
5. Thank you
6. Have a nice day

Something as simple as being respectful of others and utilizing those phrases will go a long way when dealing with others. You would be amazed how appreciative others would be to receive an occasional genuine compliment from you. Or how openly warm one becomes toward you when simply asked, "How are you doing today?" When you answer the phone, always give a greeting, introduce yourself, and then happily ask, "How may I help you?" And of course we all know to cover our mouths when we cough or sneeze, say, "Excuse me", and say, "Bless you" when others sneeze, right? Opening a door and giving a respectful gesture for the other person to enter first, will go a long way, especially for paying clients. And wait your turn before you speak, don't interrupt others and really listen when they are speaking to you, an occasional head nod to show interest and that you understand never hurts as well. Finally the golden rule always applies; *"Do unto others as you would have them do unto you."* Would it kill you to be nice to people, and what is the worst thing that can happen, they return the favor?

"How well we accomplish the exchange of these products which is observed and measured through our behavior towards each other determines our success and overall well being. The quality of our lives is in direct proportion to the quality of our interaction with all others. We make our lives better as we make other lives better, because whether they are in our homes, in our communities, on our way to work, or at work, we are all connected."
Major Lewis

Moment of Truth Opportunities to Shine

In the Introduction I stated that we all are clients of each other as well as service providers for each other. And that we exchange goods, services, thoughts, ideas, feelings, and energy, within our social exchange network through our behavior. Now I would like to expand on that idea. Can you picture yourself as the Sun (star) and center of your own solar system? Yes solar system with a sun and planets. And just as the sun resides in the center and is orbited by celestial bodies, you too are orbited by human bodies and bodies of opportunities that you are coming into contact with every day on a regular basis. This ongoing social interaction process is captured in your *moment of truth* cycle. That is when a person (client) faces you in your moment of truth opportunity window; whether that is face to face, telephonically, computer network, an email, text, tweets etc. your function is to shine bright rays of warmth and energy in the form of positive behavior as the sun gives warmth, energy and life to the earth and other orbiting bodies as depicted in figure 5.1.

Orbiting Bodies of Opportunities

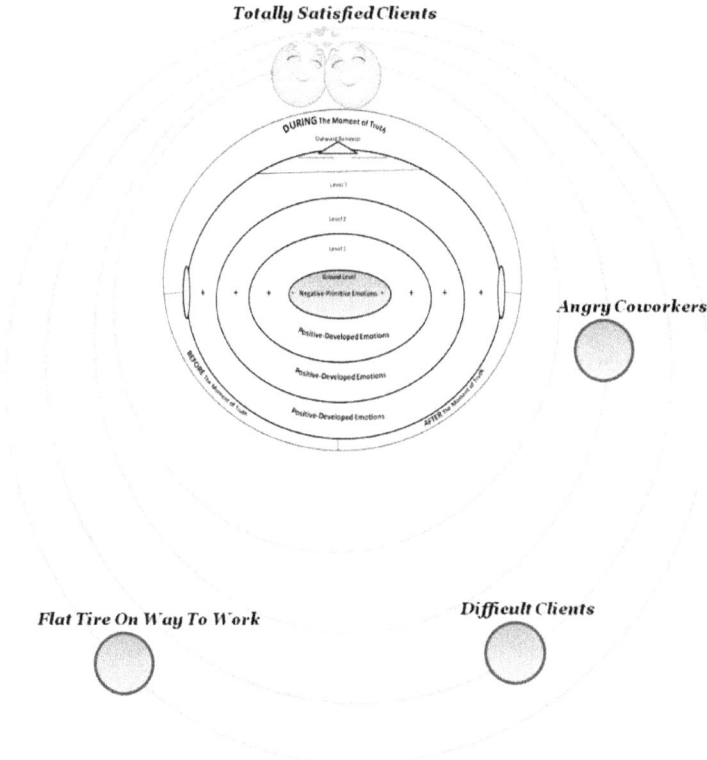

Figure 5.1

What I like about this analogy is the sun is the most powerful energy source we know and the nuclear fusion gases continuously burn at a tremendous, almost unimaginable temperature. But it has to burn that much because at the center of its core is negative gravity always pulling inward. If the sun ever stopped producing so much energy it would collapse into itself and become a black hole from the tremendous pull of gravity at its core, however without that same negative force pulling from its core the sun could not maintain its physical structure and the burning gases would just come apart and drift away in to space. It's like the illustration of figure 5.1 showing our negative emotions in the blue center held at our core always pulling always present and must always be kept under a balanced control or our socially acceptable behavior would collapse along with our positive moment of truth encounters and personal and professional relationships.

That is why we must consistently produce enough positive energy with our thoughts and emotions delivered through our behavior. As the sun we must continue producing enough positive energy in the form of showing care and concern, giving assistance, enlightenment, and great service to our solar system and shine bright to thaw even the coldest of orbiting bodies we encounter on a daily basis. Otherwise we risk being pulled into their orbit by their negative gravity being reduced to the mere properties of their orbiting moon. As for the sun, regardless of how cold and dark the earth and other planets may get while their backs are turned creating winter or night experiences for them, the powerful sun is always the sun shining bright giving warmth and positive illumination to those in its orbit.

A Matter of Focus

In other words if we lose focus of who we are and why we are there we can be negatively influenced by those with other agendas that can cause us to display behavior that is counterproductive, and even damaging to us or our primary mission. So whatever the reason you are there it is beneficial to always remember why you are doing it and keep that focus. There can be countless other people with countless other agendas around you, but keep yours in front of you. If you don't have a driving purpose for being there yet that's fine because it will be covered in later chapters.

Working with a sense of purpose and clarity will allow you to focus on maximum productivity at whatever you do, which will be highly beneficial to you and others around you. And as with the satellite/planet Pluto which completes an orbit around the sun only once every 248 years yet is still under the sun's influence, we may have clients we hardly ever see, or meet only once, yet they are a part of our system and should receive the same positive energy and great service given to those we see regularly.

We are the power that fuels our own solar system, not needing outside motivation or additional energy. We may be confronted with challenging situations during our day that are usually disintegrated upon approach like space debris. Or we can simply view as nothing more than orbiting bodies of opportunity to shine, to grow, and to know more than we did before that challenge, which is now nothing more than a part of our experiences we draw from to assist us and others in the future.

Don't sabotage your own success by adopting the phrase "that's not my job" If you have the time and skill to take care of it at the time without compromising your regular job description tasks, then do it and write it down as additional duties performed to be reviewed a later time, as in promotion or salary talks (covered in chapter 7).

Behavior Flavors

Is it possible that someone around you found your behavior to be distasteful or unpleasant in the last 24 hours at home, at work, or at the last social event you attended?

Behavior Flavors Background

As a child there were two foods that I really disliked with a passion – spinach and liver. And despite my mother changing the way she seasoned, prepared and presented them, my palate found spinach and liver most distasteful. One day my mother found a way to get me to ingest spinach. I use to love watching the cartoon Popeye the Sailor Man every day after school.

And for those of you who aren't familiar with this cartoon it was about a short and thin sailor who spent most of his time attempting to protect his girlfriend named Olive Oyl from the local bully named Bluto, who was twice the size of Popeye and very strong. So every episode Bluto would eventually bind Popeye in some way and leave him to suffer his fate while he ran off with Olive Oyl to steal a kiss. And every episode Popeye would find a way to open and ingest a can of spinach that would give him super human strength and transform him into the invincible hero the show was named after. He would then save the day and the show would end.

One day after I finished watching the cartoon my mother told me if I ate my spinach I would eventually become as strong as Popeye. And being that I had a few bullies I would have loved to lift in the air like paper bags

I reluctantly accepted her claim. Needless to say, even though spinach has great nutritional value, I never received the acclaimed super human strength, nor were the bullies impressed with my attempt to save the day. I did eat spinach for a while, but it has always been and continues to be my very last choice on a menu, and I would never purchase and cook it on my own. I still find both spinach and liver distasteful. My body has identified a dislike for those two foods and that is just a part of who I am.

Why, you may wonder, am I telling you this?

Have you ever noticed that there are people you meet socially or professionally, that you see on television, family members or associates that you just seem to dislike? And some of them could be good-hearted, well-meaning contributors to society that are good at what they do such as parents, teachers, co-workers, clergymen, or politicians. You are not a bad person and may have kept it to yourself and even tried changing your attitude toward them to no avail, because for some reason you just don't like them. And then there are those people whom you tend to gravitate toward, whom you really like a lot. You just seem to be in a better mood when you are around them or watching them on television etc. You may have just met someone and haven't even gotten to know them but like them better than people you've known for a while. Where am I going with this?

I believe that as with food, people come in different flavors as well, and are tasted through the very behavior they display to others and themselves. We all have internally, consciously or subconsciously, identified different behavior and attributes that we like and dislike in others and sometimes in ourselves. Haven't you ever described someone as being sweet or another person as being bitter? That's because you came into contact with their behavior and found aspects of it to be either tasteful or distasteful to you.

The process for determining what foods we like or dislike is this. We come into contact with the food by placing a small amount in our mouths and then we wait to hear from our taste buds as to whether we like or dislike the taste, and because each of us is unique we all *have different taste. Likewise with our emotional intellect* we are able to determine if we like or dislike physical, mental, and environmental behavior in and around us through our senses and internal gut reactions. We may not outwardly respond to, inwardly acknowledge, or even recognize the intrapersonal communication at the time, but this ongoing process is still happening.

Allow me to make the point that even though I dislike the taste of spinach myself I still understand its nutritional value, why others eat it and respect its position in the vegetable family. Likewise and because of EI skills, even though I dislike some behavior of individuals I come in contact with especially at work, I can understand them, respect their position, and work well with them despite finding some of their behavior distasteful. So we can definitely respect and cooperate with people who don't always agree with us, are different from us or who display behavior we disagree with at times. So called "difficult people" may not always be conscious of, focused on or even in control of their displayed behavior, and may not realize the bitter taste they're leaving in the emotional mouths of those around them, or the negative effects their behavior is having on other people in their environment. Ignorance is no excuse and is not always forgiven, especially in the workplace. That is why this next exercise is so important. When we ask ourselves the questions who am I and who do I want to be, we are really asking how do we presently behave and how do we want to behave in the future. After all, why do we display behavior that is counterproductive to our agendas anyway?

Behavior Flavors Menu

EXERCISE

Imagine you are sitting down in a restaurant and are handed a menu Fig 5.2. Take a minute and read through (taste) the list of behaviors below slowly, carefully one at a time and allow the different behavioral flavors to run through your emotional pallet as you perform this exercise.

Abrasive, Abusive, Active Adaptable, Aggressive, Ambitious Angry Anxious, Argumentative Assertive Assured, Belligerent, Boorish, Brave, Caring, Charming, Confident, Considerate, Cowardly, Crazy, Creepy, Cruel Careless, Cautious, Cooperative, Conceited, Conscientious, Courageous Creative, Curious, Deceitful, Dangerous, Debonair, Decisive, Defiant, Determined, Docile, Domineering Enthusiastic, Excitable, Erratic, Extroverted, Faithful, Finicky, Flashy, Flippant, Foolish, Furtive, Funny, Generous, Gracious , Guarded, Hilarious, Honorable Impulsive, Inconsiderate, Introverted, Inventive, Irritating , Jittery, Kind, Lively Malicious, Manic, Manipulative, Moody, Mysterious, Nervous, Obnoxious, Outrageous, Panicky, Pleasant, Passive, Perfectionist, Pleasant, Polite, Pompous, Pragmatic, Productive, Procrastination, Protective Quiet, Receptive Reflective, Reserved, Responsible, Romantic Rude, Secretive, Sincere, Selfish, Sensitive, Shrewd Serious, Shy, Spiteful, Strange, Thoughtful , , Thoughtless, Threatening, Trustworthy, Unsuitable, Unusual, Vengeful, Volatile, Witty, Wary, Wonderful, Zany, Zealous

Fig 5.2

1. Now utilizing intrapersonal communication skill, ask yourself which behaviors best and most accurately describe you personally and professionally in the last 24 hours or at the last social event you attended? There are no good or bad answers here, just an honest accurate self-assessment of which behaviors have been displayed in your life recently.

2. Then take a moment and think about the people you truly respect or that you admire, such as role models you aspire to be like, famous figures, success stories etc. Now identify which behaviors they have displayed.

3. Finally, identify the behaviors you would like to display in the future that you feel would represent and benefit you and those around you. You may want to write that final behavior flavors list down for future reference because it is a list of the flavors your emotional taste buds love to ingest and the behaviors that will keep you happy wherever you are and whatever the circumstances are. It's like your diet consisting of all the foods you love. This line of questioning actually helps to build and strengthen our emotional intelligence muscles and helps us take control of our lives.

Behavior Display Keypad

Figure 5.3 below is the Behavior Display Keypad I developed that captures the behaviors I've found to be most effective as a Superior Client Service Representative, as well as successfully maintaining very positive personal and professional relationships with others in my social exchange network. It is used to quickly reference and access a keypad of effective behaviors we can display as we navigate through our day confronted with orbiting bodies of opportunity. Simply press the keypad button of the displayed behavior you feel is needed to bring about the most successful positive moment of truth transactions that will benefit you and others at the time and display that behavior. As with the SMART Remote Control utilize this keypad as a quick reference focusing tool to call upon the different attributes you have available to you as you work your craft skillfully. Remember our emotions influence our behavior; they are different yet very closely related. So the presence of positive emotions makes it easier for you to choose and display the desired behavior of your choosing.

Behavior Display Keypad

Behavior Display		
Adaptable	Extroverted	Organized
Attentive	Flexible	Polite
Cheerful	Focused	Productive
Confident	Friendly	Professionalism
Consistent	Integrity	Receptive
Dependable	Motivated	Respectful
Empathetic	Open-Minded	Sincere
Enthusiastic	Optimistic	Tactful

Fig 5.3

The Behavior Display keypad and SMART Remote Control can be ordered at *www.servicesuperior.com* .

Happiness in the Workplace

At some point I usually ask those sitting in my class to raise their hands if they are happy with their jobs. Then I ask those with their hands in the air to explain why they are happy. You'd be surprised how tough this question is to answer for some people, and so I change the question slightly; how does one become happy in life generally? We could say that being very rich would make us happy, but there are too many wealthy people suffering from depression, excessively drinking and over medicating themselves looking for peace and happiness. And yes, I know what you are saying at this point; give you a shot at being wealthy, right? We could say that living forever would make us happy, but many people have lived long, and even healthy, lives but perhaps remained lonely, unfulfilled and even sad, especially at the workplace. Then I ask if the following could be in support of a happy life:

Imagine that you can see into the future, and you see that you end up a very successful person doing exactly what you love to do and being paid well for doing it. You see exactly who you are, where you are going to end up, exactly how you are going to get there, and where you are in that process today and it pleases you. Wouldn't that touch on some of the components of happiness at work, like satisfaction, contentment, sense of purpose, and an understanding of your place along the scale of your life?

A Happy Ending

Many people, especially those who are early in their employment journey, feel as though going to work is a waste of time. They aren't doing what they feel they should be doing or they aren't making the amount of money they feel they should be making. So they don't feel as though they are really a part of the mission of the company they are working for, and in the absence of motivation and satisfaction at doing something fulfilling, many people literally hate their jobs. And the emotion hate does not belong in our readily available access pool of positive emotions. Because all negative emotions attract other negative emotions and are deceiving. They make situations appear worse than they really are. Many of us like suspense in movies, but seldom appreciate it in our own lives. Abrupt surprises and unscripted narrative twists of uncertainty seem to cause us stress. Perhaps it would be less painful if we could have some up-front assurance of a happy ending.

Background

When I finished high school I didn't go straight to college. And since I still lived at home I needed to contribute financially, so I started working different jobs doing various tasks. I didn't really know what I wanted to do, but I did my best at whatever it was because I needed the money. I kept being the last one hired and the first one fired. It was becoming a little frustrating. Then an ARMY recruiter told me I can support my family, go to college, have instant credit, travel around the world, get free room and board, be trained on the latest weaponry, jump out of airplanes, and get paid for doing what I love to do. I said to myself, Major that is the life for you! So at about 21 years old, I joined the military and asked for something very exciting!

And the lesson learned that day was just because you think a job is going to be a certain way doesn't mean it has to be. And even doing a job you thought you wanted to do, not fully understanding all that the job entails doesn't ensure happiness at that job. I ended up spending forty-five days at a time playing war games in the woods in the middle of nowhere. I had to eat, sleep, and everything else in the woods, and it seemed to always rain, which made the experience wet, muddy, and cold. To make matters worse, I spent many nights standing up in a foxhole (ditch) that I had to dig myself. Or I had to sleep in a very small tent on the hard, cold and wet ground that didn't really protect me from the weather. Yes, way to go Major, way to go. Many of the other soldiers felt as miserable as I did and complained often, but once you enlist, you belong to Uncle Sam (US) for at least one term, usually three or four years. Needless to say, I was not experiencing a state of well-being characterized by emotions ranging from contentment to intense joy (happiness).

Mission

One night, as I was walking around in the woods guarding two attack helicopters, the thought struck me: since I had to be in the military for the next two years, why not make the most of it, and why not think about the great things I would be doing after I finished my tour of duty? It was dark and I was alone, so why not daydream about doing those things I felt I was really destined to do, since this obviously was a mistake and couldn't have been it, not as unhappy as I was. Even though looking back that experience uncovered my innate people skills, inner strength and leadership traits, which eventually defined

78

the rest of my life and job choices, at the time I didn't realize that.

Well, I immediately became very excited. I could hardly wait for the opportunity to pull guard duty again, rain or shine, so I could be alone and dream about and plan my future. My daydreams were in great detail and HD quality, it was like I was really there. I even started enjoying being a soldier and decided to become the best! Because once we focus on our positive emotions they bring their positive friends along and expand our hope and vision. I asked for all the available schools and training the military had to offer so I could be promoted as quickly as possible, which meant more money and decision-making, less physical work, and more management experience for my future jobs after my stint in the military.

It was amazing how excited I was when I developed a rough plan for my life which entailed an honorable discharge from the military, finding temporary employment in a technical field, meeting someone nice, getting married, having kids, and eventually going to a nine to five management job everyday, which the military was currently providing the management experience for, even though I was planning to leave. My immediate surroundings became instantly brighter. I suddenly had a purpose, and I became an active part of my company's vision and mission for success in the process. I also gained the honor and respect of many of the other soldiers that had witnessed my transformation. They even started calling me Sergeant Airborne because of my motivation, starched uniforms, shined boots, and willingness to get the job done. Without even knowing it, what I was experiencing was the power of developing and embracing a personal mission statement.

Chapter Six

Personal Mission

Personal Mission Statement

Most successful businesses utilize mission statements to define who they are, what they stand for, their objectives, and what is important to them. The mission statement allows everyone associated with the business to know its core values and goals and serves as a roadmap that allows everyone to move in the same direction in support of what is really important to the company. All major decisions must align with the company mission statement. With effective mission statements businesses attract potential investors to invest in their company because the investors believe in the company vision and see high probability for future success.

We too can believe in our own vision and see high probability for our own future success. It would be nice if we could look in the future and see exactly who we are, where we are going to end up, exactly how we are going to get there, and where we are in that process today. The closest thing to having a time machine is a Personal Mission Statement. Yes you have to do the thinking and intrapersonal communication up front and then monitor periodically, but then you would know what you want and why and how far you are from having what you want.

The interesting thing is, as we live and experience different situations we also learn more about ourselves and what we truly want and care about. It's perfectly fine to work different seemingly totally unrelated jobs until we discover our true interests and innate skills and abilities and then navigate toward what our eventual careers will be which may or may not be in the industry we are currently involved in. Just like a business mission statement, our personal mission statement allows us to define who we are and what is important to us.

Through your mission statement process you may discover that the job you currently have is what you actually would like to do and just start doing it better! You may discover that you totally enjoy making a difference in a non-professional office setting, or want to be CEO of a large corporation. You may be a Lawyer who realizes you would prefer being a Teacher, or a Security Guard who creates a personal mission statement and becomes a Secret Service Agent. All jobs in all industries need people like us to perform them. And the happier we are the better we will accomplish them.

The mission statement is our personal identification, point of reference, and becomes our personal roadmap for navigation down our successful career paths of our choosing. Our personal mission statement allows us to identify where we are on our road to success at any given time. When traveling on vacation, your map provides you with the vital information about your destination. It shows you the crossroads along the way and whether you need to take a two lane side road or the next major interstate highway. You can check your progress at each segment of the trip or make course corrections as needed along your trip and the same applies for your life with a personal mission statement.

The Journey

I love to watch the television show Star Trek. The highly advanced crews of the intergalactic space ship are able to beam to their desired destinations instantly by the press of a button in the blink of an eye. That may very well happen one day in the future but for now it is called Science Fiction. Many people want to instantaneously end up at the end of their career journey or the top of their career ladder of success in the blink of an eye, but life isn't set up that way. Just as it takes time for a seed to grow, receiving nutrients from the soil, sun and water and then being tested by the winds to become firmly rooted, we don't normally spring up the career ladder doing the perfect job receiving the perfect pay without the appropriate life challenges and achievement experiences that define us and help us grow.

I will emphasize that success is different for each of us and only after it is properly thought about and indentified within each of us can a roadmap to its destination be created. Also there is no set time allotted to discovering your ideal job other than the one you set for yourself. Some people figure out what they would like to do early in life and start working toward it immediately, while others realize what they want after discovering who they truly are. And for some, like me, their career aspirations and subsequent success targets shift and are ever-changing as they change inside through natural growth and as their lives intertwine with other people, places and situations that influence their own self awareness. Since success can be a moving target, our personal mission statements are also subject to change. However, mission statement changes should be carefully considered to ensure that they reflect true inner change in you, and not just the latest generally accepted culture or beliefs around you.

A Matter of Focus

Charting your career may entail working just for the temporary income while you also work on other supportive areas like education and training, which is the roadmap equivalent of needing to take a dirt road temporarily between major highways in route to your successful destination. Yes, you may have to temporarily perform jobs that are not what you want to do for the rest of your life, with the knowledge that it is only temporary. Therefore you can do your best and get the best experience from it today and every day, and be excited knowing it is but for a season as your new opportunity unfolds and you keep your goals clearly in front of you.

Define what success means for you first, and then you can travel your road to success one mile at a time, and take the opportunities to gain many skills that may seem trivial at the time but serve you later in your journey to your desired jobs. All jobs have generic tasks but as you bring your uniqueness to every job you do, you also receive a piece of that experience that adds to who you are and who you are becoming and will travel as a part of you for the rest of your journey.

Your personal mission statement should answer the following question: "What is my purpose?" The personal mission statement is an ongoing, living document that is modified as you learn more about yourself through living and working in different places, around different people and being faced with various situations. This accumulation of experience allows you to see who you are and who you really want to become. The more opportunities you have to apply yourself to different situations, the more you will learn about yourself and the things that are most important to you. The trick is you must fully apply yourself at each opportunity, to fully engage each challenge and create a positive track record for yourself. Be the best you at home, at work and in your community.

Always do your best no matter how insignificant you think your present circumstance or job position is. No matter how undeserving you feel your supervisor or coworkers are of your best efforts, the truth is this is not about them, but about you and the greatness within you. And since you have your positive, supportive, power emotions that will answer to you their master when called and will keep you empowered at your command, you are always one thought away from displaying your best self and leaving your unique legacy wherever you go. And you will be missed as you continue your journey of success.

Notice I'm now saying journey of success instead of journey to success. As we operate within our positive emotions, everything we do will be a successful part of the trip. And people will receive positive interactions and transactions as they encounter us.

Now that we know how to communicate with ourselves and how to access our positive emotions to support our states of well-being, we can now discover who we are today and who we would like to be tomorrow. It is easier than it may sound because once we've developed our intrapersonal communication skills from earlier chapters we can effectively ask ourselves the actual questions that really matter and hear, see, and feel the actual answers that currently exist within and around us and ultimately define who we are.

Perspective

When airplanes fly over my head or when I'm approaching a large structure like a building or a bridge, I sometimes like to do the following. I place my hand in front of my face with it facing the object and imagine myself holding the object in my hand. And it actually looks like my hand is large enough to hold the object because of the distance of the object in comparison to my hand and face. I used to do this before entering buildings for job interviews or meetings with perceived difficult clients. Holding the building in the palm of my hand gave me the sense of power and confidence instead of feeling intimidated. It's a matter of perspective and so are our lives. When you take total control over the thing you have been given the authority to control, which is yourself, you have a totally different perspective of the world around you, and you realize you are a major player in this game. Perspective is the key to staying focused on the things that really matter to you and motivated to continue to reach for them. A healthy perspective will keep you from feeling hopeless and trapped in your current situation at work, equivalent to you passing through a town on your road of success and stopping at a red light, looking around, and getting depressed thinking you live there instead of just passing through.

I like to think of our personal mission statement as our life tree that visually represents our values, beliefs and desires that reveal themselves through the choices we make and the goals we set. We should be firmly rooted in solid values and beliefs which reside beneath the surface but to which we are constantly referring as we set our goals and make our choices in life. Then as the "big bad wolves" of life huff and puff, our solid foundation holds up, and we maintain our steadfastness knowing who we are and why we chose as we did. Your personal mission statement will be revealed after you review your values, beliefs, goals, and decisions.

Values Driven

To be *values-driven* is to identify and record what is most important to you to include your core beliefs, likes and dislikes. You then have this very important information about yourself readily available as a guide as you navigate through your life. You can easily access this data as needed as your prime directive and then stay within those boundaries regulating behavior and both incoming and outgoing interactions with others. Having this values acknowledgement embedded in your decision making process minimizes decisions that contradict your core values and allow you to sleep better at night. It's like our subconscious fact-checks our day against our stored values list and reports back violations through that nagging unsettling feeling we get at times. So knowing and automatically checking our values list gives us a decisive edge when making important decisions, displaying behavior that accurately defines us best, and minimizes latter regret for decisions and actions made that contradict our core values.

Situation

For many years I have felt that if I could just make enough money that it would equate to my eventual happiness. And then I had the opportunity of holding a Senior Executive position, pretty much running the entire company and making a very comfortable salary doing so, and I was happy because of it, as far as I knew at the time. Then one day I was faced with the decision to support the company leadership, which would have meant supporting activities that directly conflicted with my personal values, morality and integrity, or the decision not to support the company, which led to my soon-to-follow state of unemployment. But the strangest thing happened as I filed for employment and sent out resumes looking for a new job. I noticed that for some reason I didn't feel unhappy, after putting so much emphasis on making a lot of money over the years. So I asked myself why was I not feeling unhappy, being unemployed during a less than booming economic period? After all, I did have a mortgage and other bills to pay, and always enjoyed eating out and buying nice things that unemployment compensation would not cover. So the question was on the table. Why was I not feeling unhappy? I then went to a nice quiet place and had an honest heart-to-head *intrapersonal* communication session and listened to myself very carefully.

Values Gut Check

After spending a few minutes in thought, I walked away with some pretty interesting information about myself. I discovered that my list of values and priorities had changed significantly over the years. And what was very important to me as a younger man was no longer dominating my life decisions. I learned that my integrity meant more to me than popularity and peer acceptance. I learned that having a loving spouse, children, family and friends that respected and supported me, meant more to my happiness than making a lucrative salary, receiving a pat on the back, or even immediate job security. Sure I had to figure out a way to produce income, but the negative emotions of fear and doubt did not paralyze me, as a victim with a clouded mind cluttered with worry and stress. In fact my negative emotions were controlled and even subdued by my more positive and supportive emotions of faith, confidence, humbleness, and purpose. And I immediately felt a sense of relief and excitement as I looked into my uncertain but hopeful and soon-to-be-focused future. My creativity began to rise, being freed after months of spending countless hours supporting the visions of others that I didn't believe in. And it was then with a peaceful mind I felt a renewed since of purpose and clarity. I chose not to fall victim to the deceptive qualities of negativity attempting to cast a shadow on the present situation. And I devoted myself to finishing this book, The Major Solution to Superior Client service, and to developing ways of helping individuals be their best selves through client service, and imparting information in support of their personal and professional growth and future successes.

Understanding and Embracing Your Values

So your values are those things which you judge to be most important in life, and what you hold to be most important to you says a lot about who you are. Values are abstract. For example, you may initially think that making a lot of money is the most important thing to you but if what first comes to mind as being important to you is something that you can hold in your hand, then you may need to think a little more about what it is that the material thing really means to you. Do you want to make a lot of money because?

- You want to be respected?
- You want to be powerful?
- You want to be appreciated?
- You want others to love you?
- You want to be free of financial worry, why?

List of Values

Abundance, Acceptance, Accomplishment, Achievement, Acknowledgement, Affluence, Appreciation, Approachability, Attractiveness, Awareness, Balance, Being the best, Belonging, Control, Education, Excellence, Excitement, Experience, Exploration, Expressiveness, Extroversion, Exuberance, Fairness, Faith, Fame, Family, Fidelity, Fierceness, Financial independence, Fitness, Freedom, Fun, Growth, Guidance, Happiness, Harmony, Health, Independence, Integrity, Intimacy, Introversion, Investing, Joy; Justice, Knowledge, Motivation, Perfection, Popularity, Power, Relaxation, Reliability, Respect, Satisfaction, Security, Self-control, Sexuality, Silence, Silliness, Spirituality, Spontaneity, Success, Support, Wealth, Winning, Wisdom

EXERCISE

Take a look at the above list of values and choose the 5 that are most important to you at this time. This list is not all-inclusive. If values that come to mind for you are not on this list, that's okay, just add them to the list.

Then write those five down in the order of priority with 1 being the most important:

1.

2.

3.

4.

5.

Creating Your Goals

Now you are able to create a list of goals that supports your values and your mission statement. Setting values-centered goals is a very effective strategy for successful professionals but also for all people in their everyday lives. I have always taught that a person can measure their maturity by the decisions they make, but if a person has never asked themselves what is important to them, how can they make a meaningful decision when faced with a new situation?

If being true to your word is important to you and you make a promise, but then something else comes up that causes you to revise your plans, you can make your decision without a lot of searching and using time better spent elsewhere. Being law-abiding citizens is important to many people, and when they are faced with decisions regarding making a profit that might include breaking the law, questions of maturity and one's personal integrity must be included in the considerations.

That is when they need to mentally prioritize their options against their values list to make the best decision for them; even if they face opposition they know this is what's best for them individually. Values-centered goals make important decisions easier and sounder, not to mention easier to live with, in the long run. If you know your values and you have goals that reflect those values, your decisions will also reflect those values and you will sleep better as stated above.

EXERCISE

Let's start by asking the question, what do I want to have or have achieved by a certain age? Some common age specific goals are:

- Earning a diploma, certification or degree
- Moving into an apartment or buying a house
- Owning or leasing a car
- Having a certain job or income level
- Having a certain savings amount
- Traveling
- Marriage
- Children
- Steady income
- Healthy diet, fitness level or targeted weight
- Financial independence
- Retired by a certain age etc

Creating, recording, and viewing goals by a certain age on an actual age chart can be highly motivating, sobering, and very effective in refocusing our priorities as we see what we want in relation to where we are on the age chart figure 6.1.

1. Write each goal on your wish list in the appropriate box in figure 6.2 and record your target year and age. Once you record a goal in the top section it becomes a project with you as the Project Manager (PM). As such you are to set realistic goals and realistic target completion dates. Allow yourself timeline flexibility. As with any successful project the dates can be revised as needed.

2. Once you record your goal think about what action items you need to perform in order to make that goal a reality and list each step of the process as a project task for that specific goal/project. Make sure you calculate and record a start date and a finish date for each individual task needing to be accomplished. This is the model so feel free to transfer your projects to mediums such as graph paper, excel, a calendar or project management software, whichever is most effective for you.

3. After you've charted your goals sign your name below as a self-commitment to see your projects through. Whichever goals you do set as you complete them or come closer to them by completing the individual tasks, you will feel a sense of accomplishment which will make you happier than someone who has not set goals. And you will perform better and treat others better as you feel better about yourself. Because you are your biggest client we are doing all this to please you and make you happy. And that puts you closer to our goal of *superior client support* for others!

Values Centered Goal Charting

| 18 20 | 25 | 30 | 35 | 40 | 45 | 50 | 55 | 60 | 65 | 70 | 75 | 80 | 85 | 90 | 95 | 100 |

Fig 6.1

YEAR_____. AGE__	YEAR_____. AGE__	YEAR_____. AGE__	YEAR_____. AGE__	YEAR_____. AGE__
GOAL 1:_____	GOAL 1:_____	GOAL 1:_____	GOAL 1:_____	GOAL 1:_____
GOAL 2:_____	GOAL 2:_____	GOAL 2:_____	GOAL 2:_____	GOAL 2:_____
GOAL 3:_____	GOAL 3:_____	GOAL 3:_____	GOAL 3:_____	GOAL 3:_____
GOAL 4:_____	GOAL 4:_____	GOAL 4:_____	GOAL 4:_____	GOAL 4:_____
GOAL 5:_____	GOAL 5:_____	GOAL 5:_____	GOAL 5:_____	GOAL 5:_____
GOAL 6:_____	GOAL 6:_____	GOAL 6:_____	GOAL 6:_____	GOAL 6:_____

GOAL 1 PROJECT TASK	TARGET DATE Start/Finish	GOAL 1 PROJECT TASK	TARGET DATE Start/Finish	GOAL 1 PROJECT TASK	TARGET DATE Start/Finish	GOAL 1 PROJECT TASK	TARGET DATE Start/Finish	GOAL 1 PROJECT TASK	TARGET DATE Start/Finish
1		1		1		1		1	
2		2		2		2		2	
3		3		3		3		3	
4		4		4		4		4	
5		5		5		5		5	

GOAL 2 PROJECT TASK	TARGET DATE Start/Finish	GOAL 2 PROJECT TASK	TARGET DATE Start/Finish	GOAL 2 PROJECT TASK	TARGET DATE Start/Finish	GOAL 2 PROJECT TASK	TARGET DATE Start/Finish	GOAL 2 PROJECT TASK	TARGET DATE Start/Finish
1		1		1		1		1	
2		2		2		2		2	
3		3		3		3		3	
4		4		4		4		4	
5		5		5		5		5	

GOAL 3 PROJECT TASK	TARGET DATE Start/Finish	GOAL 3 PROJECT TASK	TARGET DATE Start/Finish	GOAL 3 PROJECT TASK	TARGET DATE Start/Finish	GOAL 3 PROJECT TASK	TARGET DATE Start/Finish	GOAL 3 PROJECT TASK	TARGET DATE Start/Finish
1		1		1		1		1	
2		2		2		2		2	
3		3		3		3		3	
4		4		4		4		4	
5		5		5		5		5	

GOAL 4 PROJECT TASK	TARGET DATE Start/Finish	GOAL 4 PROJECT TASK	TARGET DATE Start/Finish	GOAL 4 PROJECT TASK	TARGET DATE Start/Finish	GOAL 4 PROJECT TASK	TARGET DATE Start/Finish	GOAL 4 PROJECT TASK	TARGET DATE Start/Finish
1		1		1		1		1	
2		2		2		2		2	
3		3		3		3		3	
4		4		4		4		4	
5		5		5		5		5	

GOAL 5 PROJECT TASK	TARGET DATE Start/Finish	GOAL 5 PROJECT TASK	TARGET DATE Start/Finish	GOAL 5 PROJECT TASK	TARGET DATE Start/Finish	GOAL 5 PROJECT TASK	TARGET DATE Start/Finish	GOAL 5 PROJECT TASK	TARGET DATE Start/Finish
1		1		1		1		1	
2		2		2		2		2	
3		3		3		3		3	
4		4		4		4		4	
5		5		5		5		5	

GOAL 6 PROJECT TASK	TARGET DATE Start/Finish	GOAL 6 PROJECT TASK	TARGET DATE Start/Finish	GOAL 6 PROJECT TASK	TARGET DATE Start/Finish	GOAL 6 PROJECT TASK	TARGET DATE Start/Finish	GOAL 6 PROJECT TASK	TARGET DATE Start/Finish
1		1		1		1		1	
2		2		2		2		2	
3		3		3		3		3	
4		4		4		4		4	
5		5		5		5		5	

Fig 6.2

I will complete each project to the best of my abilities.
Yours Truly, _____. Project Manager

Recording your Personal Mission Statement

By now you should be pretty familiar with yourself, your wants, ambitions, likes and dislikes, in short what makes you tick. I have found it to be easier to first identify your values and beliefs, and then chart your goals in order to gain a clearer portrait of yourself. Then write a sentence or a small paragraph that reflects what is your purpose or mission?

If you are younger toward the left side of the above age chart you may not have as much to say about yourself as someone further to the right on the age chart. Since your mission statement is revisited and updated regularly it will expand as you are exposed to more situations that will both expand you and reveal more about you. Feel free to look at examples of personal mission statements, but yours will be unique to you. Refer back to chapter 5 and the behavior you admired in others you respect and that you wanted displayed in your own life.

Finally you may want a statement about you to include words like: I value, I believe, I want, I want to, or I will, which follow this chapter's progression, and maybe even a phrase beginning with "I want to help", etc. Following are some examples of personal mission statements to get you started:

- *I will act respectfully in all circumstances, love my family unconditionally, follow my dreams despite peer pressure, and laugh as often as possible.*
- *I want to really know myself first and to help others. I will focus on my health and creating a*

better environment for my family and friends. I will show more care and concern for those I care about. I will increase my income while fulfilling my dream of teaching.

- *I want to be the best I can be with the time I have. I want to use my talent of music to make a good living and provide much enjoyment for others. I want to have a family, love and protect them, and provide a role model they can learn from and be proud of.*
- *My purpose for being on this earth is to help others develop their abilities, and to show love and compassion for those less fortunate than myself. I believe in karma and I will strive to keep mine as positive as possible.*
- *To honor my body and fulfill my purpose of showing others how to eat healthy and stay fit. To stay connected with my children and always be there to assist them or just available to listen.*
- *I will treat everyone with the same respect regardless of race or gender. I believe I am a part of a larger community and will strive to contribute by encouraging and supporting the dreams and aspirations of others.*
- *To find happiness and peace of mind. I seek to experience all that life has for me and to take full advantage of my experiences. I wish to enjoy the love and respect of my family, friends, and business associates.*

So write your statement and remember there is no wrong personal mission statement if it honestly reflects you and/or how you would like to be remembered.

Personal Mission Statement

_____
_____
_____
_____
_____
_____
_____
_____
_____
_____
_____
_____
_____
_____
_____
_____
_____
_____
_____
_____
_____
_____
_____
_____
_____
_____.

Part 2

Superior
Job
Performance

Chapter Seven

Making the Most of Your Technical Skills

"Being busy does not always mean real work. The object of all work is production or accomplishment and to either of these ends there must be forethought, system, planning, intelligence, and honest purpose, as well as perspiration. Seeming to do is not doing."

Thomas A. Edison

Systems

Systems are all around us and are a part of our very existence. From the solar system, economic system, political system, ecological system, energy systems, educational systems, etc. We would be in big trouble if some of those systems or parts of those systems mentioned were to stop functioning. And yet there are others that affect us more closely, like our computer system, transportation system, and our communication system. We scream bloody murder when these don't function properly. And of course there are even more personal systems, such as the digestive system, endocrine system, or immune system. We're in big trouble if they decide to take a day off or show up late.

A very basic business definition of a system is a set of methods, procedures, and routines established to perform a duty or solve a problem. Why the focus on systems? Consider with all these systems in and around us, we would be totally out of sync with our universe if we were without a system ourselves, yet we spend our entire lives working , living, and being affected by so many of them every day. We all have systems we automatically follow without thinking about them as systems. After awakening each morning we have personal morning routines/systems with a process that might resemble this as charted in figure 7.1.:

1. Shut off the alarm
2. Get out of bed
3. Use the restroom
4. Brush our teeth
5. Take a shower

6.　　Get dressed
7.　　Eat breakfast
8.　　Leave the house

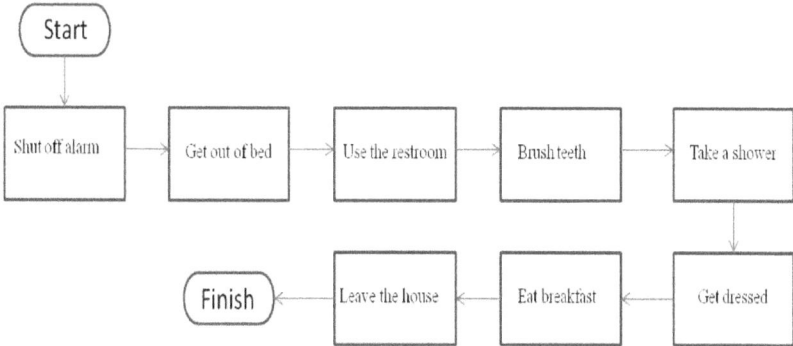

```
  ( Start )
      |
      v
+-------------+   +--------------+   +----------------+   +-------------+   +---------------+
| Shut off    |-->| Get out of   |-->| Use the        |-->| Brush teeth |-->| Take a shower |
| alarm       |   | bed          |   | restroom       |   |             |   |               |
+-------------+   +--------------+   +----------------+   +-------------+   +---------------+
                                                                                    |
                                                                                    v
              ( Finish )<--+ Leave the house +<--+ Eat breakfast +<--+ Get dressed +
```

Fig 7.1

And we've gotten pretty good at that routine. It has become automatic and we even do it while half asleep. The better we execute that morning routine the better our morning tends to be. And a failure at a point in that process can definitely affect our morning. Say the alarm doesn't ring. Most of us have experienced that at some point. When that occurs, we are left scrambling trying to make up for that failed or poorly executed system process step and even skipping other steps in the process so our next system such as transit system or employment isn't drastically affected by that last one.

Now in terms of our work lives, we need a reliable system or routine so that no matter what tasking we are responsible for completing, we won't be like the underperforming alarm in step one of figure 7.1 that ended up affecting the rest of the larger process it was associated with. We are also a part of larger systems while at work, and should avoid doing to them what a malfunctioning cell phone or, worse, an underperforming digestive system does to us. In other words, by identifying and utilizing our own system we avoid being the weak link in the product or service supply chain of which we are a part, and by which we make our living.

Personal Performance Management System

We should have a personal performance management system for the successful completion of our job description processes and related activities regardless of the industry, level or position. We should be able to quickly perform, document, assess the quality of, make any needed adjustments to, and complete the process tasks successfully before anyone else has to become involved or comment on our performance except to praise us for a great job, and eventually pay us the best rate possible for a job well done! When we're able to repeatedly follow that routine automatically, we have established our own successful performance management system with accuracy and consistency, working wherever and within whatever larger organizational system we are a part, no matter how effective or lacking that larger system may be. In a sense you are www.yourself.com representing yourself despite whoever else you are working for or with.

Always put your best foot forward, and your quality brand on whatever tasks you complete, because you never know who is watching from a distance, or even from right in front of you. They could very well be your next great break or unforeseen opportunity. *Making the best of your technical skills* is really about self performance management. As in the previous chapter, you were the "PM" managing your own personal goals and treating them as mini projects, in this chapter we will break your job description down into manageable chunks that, like your morning routine at home, you can perform with quality and ease, and without supervision.

It can be very effective to view everything we do as a process or as a series of processes. This allows us to effectively divide them into individual process steps or tasks that can be:

1.   Easily managed
2.   Observed and Measured
3.   Improved upon
4.   Reproduced consistently

We do this by viewing each job description item as a process with a logical flowchart with clearly defined start and finish points. The activities that make up each job description item can be sequentially and graphically depicted, breaking that process down into individual tasks that can be managed individually or even broken down into sub-tasks as needed. Once each process is fully understood, we can meet or exceed our own established process standards that will be discussed later.

If we interacted with any internal or external clients during that process or task, was it a positive *moment of truth* experience by both? If not, then why and how can we improve the quality of our exchange? And that's it. We use our personal performance management plan to mentally record that information, note needed adjustments, make adjustments and rate our success. This all becomes a simple mental exercise in time and your personal performance management system will be automatic. Your great brand and reputation will accompany you wherever you go and in whatever you do.

All you need to do is:

1. Obtain your current job description as soon as possible, and add all the additional tasks you are expected to perform that don't appear on that job description.
2. Document your work as you perform it and email it to your management for approval as your job description if there is no job description available.
3. Obtain a copy of your organization performance evaluation so you can ensure you have listed all the technical criteria necessary to exceed the expectations of the larger organizational system you are a part of, and which you will ultimately be judged.

Your tasks will get easier as you work them and you will perform them better and more quickly. The law of efficiency will cause additional work to come your way, which is a good thing if handled correctly. For you to receive more work than a counterpart may seem unfair initially but don't complain. The rule of 80% of the work being performed by 20% of the people will manifest itself. Management naturally drifts to dependable quality and that's what you want. Quality is your brand. Since you have a copy of your job description, you need to document all new tasking that doesn't appear on the initial job description to prevent scope creep, which is when a poorly detailed job description starts to grow out of control unreasonably. You can present this documented additional workload at your next performance review as solid justification for additional pay or promotion.

Personal Performance Management System

Adaptability

Time never stops, which equals *moments of truth* and *moments of opportunity*. Sleepwalking through your career and becoming complacent, performing the same tasks and fighting change is very counterproductive and that view must be abandoned immediately. Otherwise you will become obsolete and useless as time ticks on in an ever-evolving world of moving systems with moving parts. Adaptability is the key here, so revisit your goals list from the previous chapter often as you see the need for education and training and accept the new challenges as they become available.

A Matter of Focus

If you somehow slipped through the preschool age social compliance process of sharing and working well with others, or didn't embrace chapters 1 through 5 of this book, then you are a weak link in the system and it's time for you to grow up. The average person spends more time at work with coworkers than with anyone else. So you and they are interdependent components of the organizational system, which is one of many reasons getting along with each other is vital to the success of you all. You and your coworkers are codependent internal clients as explained in chapter 2 the business process section, and will be judged on your work performance regardless of whether you like each other or not. So your primary goal here is not to win a popularity contest but to perform as a winning team – or losing team – the choice is yours.

When we have a performance management plan we keep our focus on the successful completion of the interrelated processes regardless of secondary topics like personality compatibility. You are an organ within an organism. Many chronic diseases are caused by the immune system. It malfunctions and fails to recognize its interdependent associated system organs of the body and attacks them. Organism sounds like organization and your real enemy to attack is not your co-workers but inconsistent quality products and services that result from not focusing on your personal performance management system, which creates problems for the organizational body as a whole.

I joined the military at 21 years old, which I thought was pretty young, but as it turned out there were soldiers there as young as 17. My first few weeks were not easy. And I had to adapt to a totally new and challenging environment quickly in order to endure it. There were people there from all over the United States, places I had never even heard of. The recruits were totally different ages, races, cultures, religions, social status, and economic levels.

As we all looked at each other the feelings of fear, distrust and unfamiliarity seemed to be in the air, until we met the Drill Sergeant who clearly represented the overwhelming immediate threat to our calm existence. And even though we still were unfamiliar with each other, we all agreed that this guy's mission was to ruin our day, and we began to unite with each other.

The several hundred people were divided into units and the units were divided into platoons consisting of about forty people. There was a very intimidating, aggressive and demanding Drill Sergeant assigned to each platoon. Then the Drill Sergeants looked among the recruits and started assigning us as Platoon leaders to supervise those forty people, and get blamed for their screw-ups. I remember thinking I wouldn't want to be the poor sap in charge of this group of derelicts that just met each other from everywhere with very little in common and no incentive to work well together. And then of course I was chosen to be that guy.

Having a high degree of EI, I quickly realized the term "The military will make you or break you" was about adaptability and being flexible enough to bend to new situations, challenges and ideas. The Drill Sergeant felt he could depend on me and I, in turn, chose four Squad Leaders I thought I could depend on to manage teams consisting of ten personnel each.

So the Drill Sergeant would call me to the office and give me tasks and information for the platoon, and I passed it on accordingly and solicited platoon compliance. If and when just one person out of the forty failed, we all paid the price by doing strenuous physical training before dawn and during inclement weather, which turned out to be for our benefit, because in the event we had to serve our country in an armed conflict on the battlefield physical conditioning and adverse weather condition adaptability are very much welcomed. But at the time it seemed a heavy price to pay for just one person missing the mark.

"Don't lower your expectations to meet your performance. Raise your level of performance to meet your expectations. Expect the best of yourself, and then do what is necessary to make it a reality."

Ralph Marston

Your Manager Is Not the Enemy

Since then I've had the pleasure of managing many military and civilian teams, large and small, and they've all had a few things in common:

1. There was a mission.
2. There was a chain of command.
3. The missions were broken down to manageable individual tasks.

I was fortunate to learn early in my career that managing is mainly the ability to observe, measure, and motivate performance in others. Your manager does not lay awake at night plotting your demise; he or she is simply trying to feed their family. Your manager's performance is determined by *your* performance. There is always a mission to perform, and your lackluster output is their lackluster ability to motivate you to perform at a higher level. Likewise, your high performance output helps to feed their family as they are compensated for a job well done, and they will be indebted and appreciative for you making them look good. This appreciation for you will come in the form of job security and higher pay, because high performers are paid more and are more successful overall than low or mediocre performers in every industry. If you are not a high performer, your real enemy is the lack of skill, focus, or motivation, all of which are readily available and obtainable.

The technical aspect of our scale model is a lot easier to observe and measure than the communication side. Technical performance is the repeated, near-flawless execution of the tasks assigned to you that your organization needs done to perform its mission successfully, end of story. If this is not being done you are either currently unable or unwilling to do it, and either way, there is someone else in need of a job that is willing and able to do it within the allotted specifications required. It may sound cold, but that is the left brain, literal, results-driven orientation side of the scale. If you purchase a high performance vehicle that claims to accelerate from 0 to 60 mph in 5.5 seconds then that is what result you require. And the first time that doesn't happen, you would be at the car dealer bright and early expecting an adjustment, a replacement, or your money back, right? And that is the technical side of the scale.

The Major Solution Scale Balance

Performance   Communication
Results   Skills

Left Brain   Right Brain

Fig 7.2

Technical Skills

Now that we have built up a solid communications skills platform in previous chapters let's break down any job into manageable parts so that you can achieve improvement, starting with developing a true understanding of your technical skills, and exactly what technical skills are required in your current position.

Let's define what we mean by your technical skills first. Your job description duties and responsibilities are what you are required to do for your organization for pay. Your technical skills are the talent and expertise you possess, and the knowledge, training, and experience you draw from to successfully perform the processes and physical step-by-step job description duties and responsibilities. For instance, if you work in a service department of an organization and if one of your job responsibilities is to receive client service calls, then that is a process with individual tasks that may look like this:

1) Answer calls in priority order
2) Listen to client problem or request
3) Access and update the client database used by your organization and generate a ticket
4) Assess and assign ticket to proper department
5) Update caller with resolution or ticket number to track progress of request

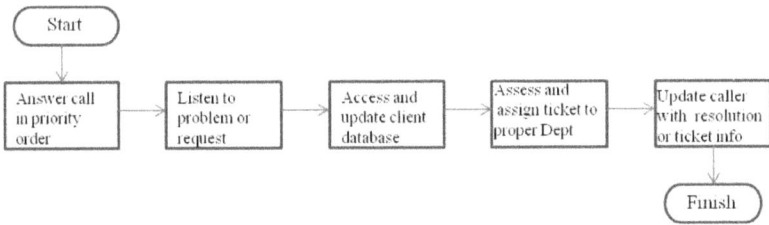

Fig 7.3

After you have accomplished this set of tasks to fulfill this part of your job description several times, these tasks become easier and you can perform them quickly and more proficiently. After you have yet more experience and even some specialized training with this portion of your job description, you can train others on how to perform the same tasks because you now possess a high enough technical skill level, which could be a measure of your proficiency at your next performance evaluation.

During a performance evaluation, your manager or supervisor will review your skill level and give their interpretation of how well you have executed the tasks that were assigned to you, which puts your performance on full display after the fact. Having your own performance management routine keeps those tasks on display between reviews, like having a reality show camera man following you around. It has been proven that overall productivity and even moral behavior are raised when people think they are being observed and measured, which is a positive attribute of your system. So incorporating self-observation and measurement in your daily activities is very beneficial to increasing and maintaining high performance.

113

"When you change the way you look at things, the things you look at change."
Dr Wayne Dyer

Observation and Measurement

I have always been intrigued and excited by Quantum Mechanics mainly because of the Quantum Physicist's bottom-up approach of revealing how everything in the universe really works. They have shown that the entire universe and *everything* in it, to include us, are made up of tiny molecules called atoms. And then they discovered that those atoms are made up of yet smaller particles, which really gets exciting! Quantum Physicists have broken existence down to its most fundamental state in order to understand the vastness of it all.

What is most interesting is how these tiny particles which are the building blocks of all matter behave when being observed and measured. When left alone these particles are in a state of flux and could be located anywhere in the universe. This is called a probability wave because they could be in one or all of many possible locations and connected like an ocean wave. But when they are observed and measured by some type of instrument they lock into one fixed location exactly where you look for them to be, and that is amazing. It gets much weirder but for our purpose we will stop at the fact that research has proven that the tiny particles that make up the atoms that we, and all matter in the universe are made from, exist in many possible states until observed and measured, when they then change and appear where you look for them.

As with quantum mechanics I have always taken things apart to see how they worked, and on occasions couldn't get them back together. And I didn't stop with material things but with concepts, behavior, relationships, processes and whatever seems complicated but looks like it can be taken apart or broken down to its most fundamental state where it could be observed and measured for understanding, because I believe anything we can really understand we can improve upon, or be improved by.

However, here I am focusing on the *observer effect* which refers to changes that the act of observation and measurement will make on a thing being observed. In thermodynamics, a standard mercury-in-glass thermometer must absorb or give up some thermal energy to record a temperature, and therefore changes the temperature of the body which it is measuring. Or how you change a circuit's current with a voltmeter just by connecting the voltmeter to the circuit for a measurement, or how you let a little air out of a tire when you attempt to check it with a tire gauge. The observer effect is also present with people and activities. People behave differently when they are aware of being watched. The very act of the observation and measurement causes a change in whatever is being measured.

The Observer Effect at Home

One day I walked into my bedroom after thinking about the quantum probability wave theory, which suggests a material object doesn't have to have physical form until someone looks at it, when it then appears where the observer looks for it. So I sat on my bed and looked directly at this picture on my wall. Now I kind of see this picture in my peripheral vision every time I walk into the room but never actually stopped and focused on it. But this day when I did I was amazed at how beautiful it was and the longer I observed the picture the more alive it seemed to become, as if its total job was to bring me beauty when I looked for and expected it. It got a little weird, when as soon as I began to turn from the picture it began to lose its beauty and purpose, becoming vague and fading in my peripheral vision. Not until I focused directly on it again did it take a definite form and give the beautiful detail to fulfill its expected purpose.

Then my mind shifted gears to when I had become very interested in a particular model of car and was considering purchasing it, how that model car started showing up all over town throughout my day. They had to have always been there, but only in a peripheral vagueness like the picture that has always been but out of my focus. I am told this happens when you get pregnant too – suddenly there are pregnant people everywhere!

The Observer Effect at Work

Can we extend that chain of thinking to our job responsibilities that we really should be paying attention to? Perhaps we go through the motions of our day vaguely interacting with our assigned tasks but only viewing them in our peripheral vision with lackluster execution and not expecting and therefore not receiving the full intended function or purpose at the time. And only when something goes wrong, as with the alarm clock not ringing in the morning, do we focus on the task reactively. Then we look back at our performance of those job responsibilities, say during a performance review, which may not be as fulfilling or beneficial as it could have been if we had fully engaged those tasks, like staring directly at the beautiful picture on the wall with the focus and expectation the observer effect demands. Or we may have even changed our level of execution of the task through observation and measurement as with the thermometer or voltmeter above.

Now I see a *performance probability wave* which means that at any given time our rate of performance execution of a particular task could be anywhere from very low to extremely high. Sometimes we do the activity well and sometimes we don't, until we lock it in, observe, measure, and change it. And maybe as we express interest in improving that specific task our minds can open up to all the associated opportunities to support improvement, like casual reading or available training that will start showing up all over the place like that model of car did after I expressed committed interest in purchasing one.

So how do we remember to fully engage the daily tasks we are responsible for, receive the benefits of the observation and measurement effect, and increase our performance of those tasks we deem necessary to become a high performer, without spending our entire days recording steps and redesigning all our processes in the pursuit of increasing our overall effectiveness? I'm glad you asked!

The Task Performance Meter

Task Performance Meter			
Current Task	L	M	H
Knowledge			✓
Quality			✓
Quantity			✓
Initiative			✓
Adaptability			✓
Timeliness			✓

Increase Performance

Performance Steps	TARGET DATE Start Finish
1	
2	
3	

Fig 7.4

This performance meter works like any other meter that observes and measures output such as the voltmeter mentioned above. It is a mental tool to help you focus on raising your performance output by concentrating on individual tasks vs. attempting to control many processes at once. It's much easier and more effective to keep track of one item instead of several simultaneously. The acronym to remember the task performance meter process is OMI, pronounced (*Oh My!*), which are the 3 steps to high performance output: Observation, Measurement, and Increase performance (OMI).

The Task Performance Meter consists of the 3 OMI sections shown in figure 7.5.

➢ Section 1 is the Observation section which would contain the task to be observed.

➤ Section 2 is the Measurement section listing the measurement categories and the gauge levels low, medium, and high, with the end desired high-level performance output already completed with check markings.

➤ Section 3 is the Increase Performance section with a path to high performance achievement area.

So the only thing left for you to do is to take the current task execution measurement and decide the path to high performance and that's it. Oh My! Have an updated copy of your job description and organization performance evaluation on hand to refer to as discussed earlier in this chapter, and now you are ready to be both the observer and the observed participant. So considering the difference that is made to an activity or a person by it being observed, you are now your own change agent and job performance manager. And you began each experiment with the desired high performance results in mind.

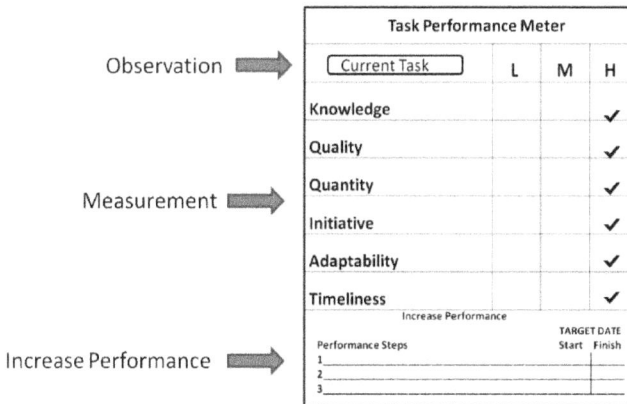

Fig 7.5

Break job description down to its smallest component/task.

EXERCISE

Now let's take a look at our client service department job description depicted in figure 7.6 below. Read the first line of your job description and see the process map in your mind or map it out on paper or computer, whichever works best for you.

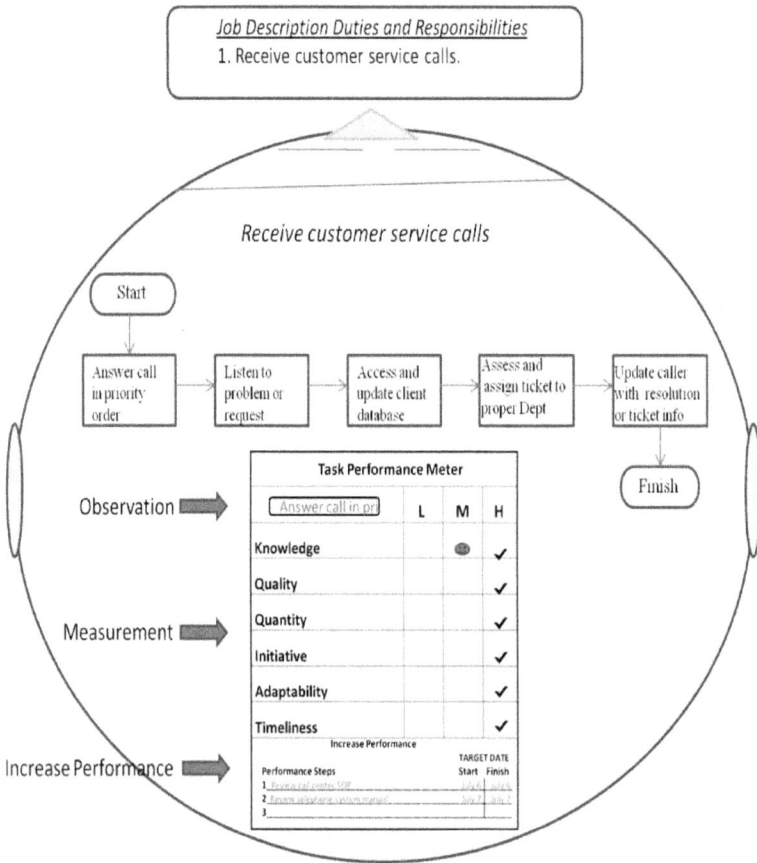

Fig 7.6

This illustration shows everything inside the head because you should be able to complete the OMI process mentally after a few practice times, if not break the task down into the lowest sub-task possible.

Step 1: Hold the Task Performance Meter in your hand and mentally place the first task of the first job description process in the Task Window for observation as if it is being examined under a microscope. In our example case it would be: *Answer call in priority order,* as shown in the first activity box of the process map above. This step could be thought of as pulling the task out of the *performance probability wave* mentioned earlier and locking it into a definite position ready to be measured and changed, instead of mindlessly going through the motions and vaguely seeing the task in your peripheral vision along with countless other random thoughts.

Step 2: Measure your performance against the *high* performance standard checked for each category starting with the knowledge category. Get in touch with your biggest critic – who is you, if you're like most people – and honestly ask yourself; do you have a *high level* of knowledge for this task? If the answer is yes, you move to the next category of Quality, and if the answer is no, move to step 3 and think of a few ways to increase your knowledge of that task. So for this example you may feel you have a medium knowledge of, say, the company's standard operating procedures (SOP) for service calls, or you may not be totally versed on all the functions of the telephone system being used, or maybe you have room for growth with your speaking or vocabulary skills.

Step 3: Identify ways to increase your performance for this task category.

For this example you may consider obtaining a copy of the company SOP for service calls, or consider reading the telephone system operator's manual and taking an English course, or just studying vocabulary words while relaxing. Keep these short and simple, so the chances of completion will be greater. There is no set time period or set number of tasks or categories that have to be done at once. This is at your own pace because you are the observer/evaluator and performance manager. Your mind will effortlessly work on issues you've identified in the background while you go about your daily routine. And you won't become defensive or feel the pressure associated with being judged by someone other than you. Fig 7.6 shows the complete OMI process.

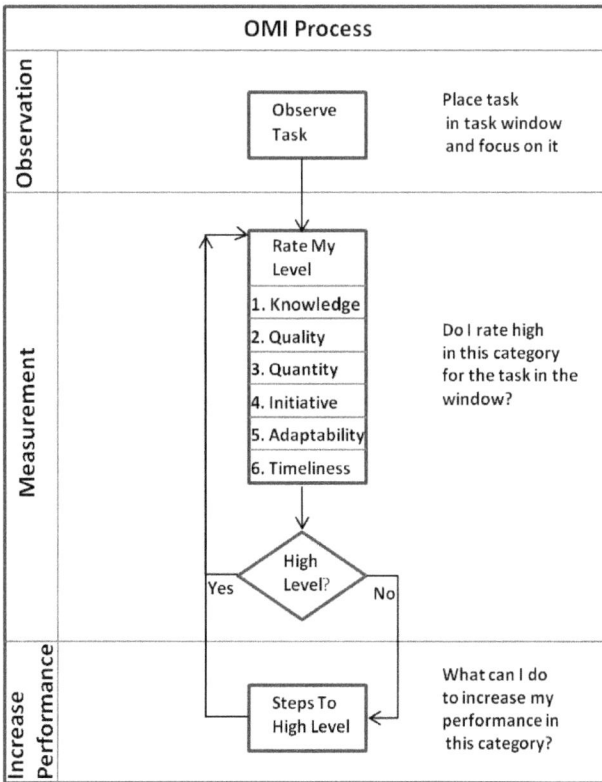

Fig 7.6

Job descriptions are made up of individual processes, and processes are made up of individual tasks. Your high performance task execution ensures the high performance of their associated processes, which makes you a *high performer* as the process owner. We have now completely covered the two sides of the scale, communications side and technical side. And we now have the mental tools to focus on each side.

To maintain Service Superior balance **The SMART Remote Control,** covered in chapter 4, is our communications or emotional intelligence (EI) tool and the **Task Performance Meter** is our technical skills tool as depicted below in figure 7.7.

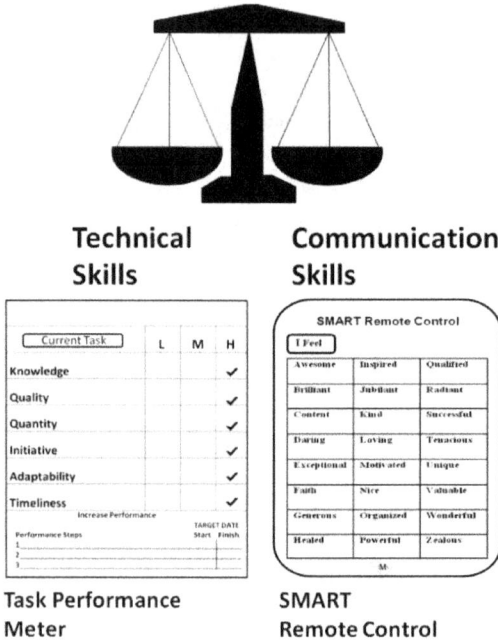

Fig 7.7

The SMART Remote Control is also our *internal* tool for emotions control and **The Behavior Display Keypad** covered in chapter 5 is our *external* tool for behavior control displayed to others as depicted below in Fig. 7.8.

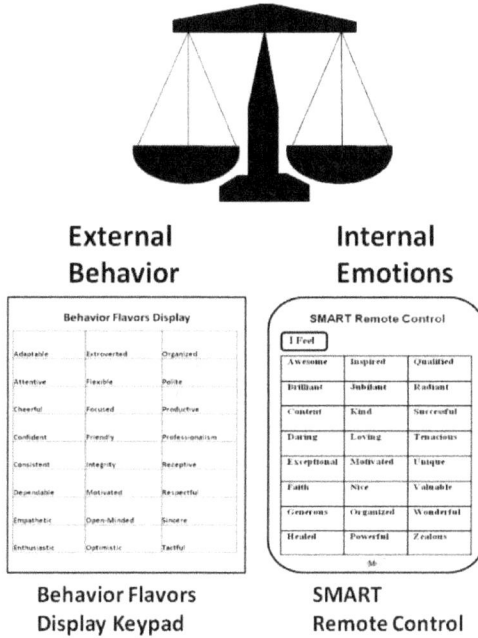

External Behavior — Internal Emotions

Behavior Flavors Display		
Adaptable	Extroverted	Organized
Attentive	Flexible	Polite
Cheerful	Focused	Productive
Confident	Friendly	Professionalism
Consistent	Integrity	Receptive
Dependable	Motivated	Respectful
Empathetic	Open-Minded	Sincere
Enthusiastic	Optimistic	Tactful

Behavior Flavors Display Keypad

SMART Remote Control		
I Feel		
Awesome	Inspired	Qualified
Brilliant	Jubilant	Radiant
Content	Kind	Successful
Daring	Loving	Tenacious
Exceptional	Motivated	Unique
Faith	Nice	Valuable
Generous	Organized	Wonderful
Healed	Powerful	Zealous
Me		

SMART Remote Control

Fig 7.8

These mental tools are in the form of Smart cards that fit in the palm of your hand that can be carried around during the day and are available at www.servicesuperior.com.

Now that we have our tools let's put it all together in chapter 8 *Putting It All Together; the Moment of Truth Cycles.*

Part3

Superior
Client
Service
Application

Chapter Eight

Putting It All Together; the Moment of Truth Cycles

This is the part where we put it all together in a nice neat package that we can remember and repeat as often as necessary. It is a model that incorporates the various tools covered in previous chapters, and that fits into our daily routine. In order to accomplish this we need to utilize the power of cycles.

The Power of Cycles

Cycles are part of our everyday lives, of course, and indeed all of existence contains cycles within cycles — from something as small as particles to as great as the orbit of celestial bodies. The cycle of birth, growth, and death are operative within all our lives, and the twenty-four hours connecting each day, the days connecting weeks, the weeks connecting months and the four seasons connecting the years are examples of cycles crucial to our existence. Our daily cycle of time determines what we should be eating, where we should be and even what we should be doing accordingly. And even the business cycle plays a large part in when to invest or not to invest our money in the financial markets. *A cycle is an observed, regularly repeated sequence of events.* There are times I wake up in the middle of the night with a stomach ache or similar discomfort but thanks to cycle awareness I can feel at ease knowing that morning will swing around faithfully on time and I will probably feel better or at least the world will look a little better to me as the morning sun shines through my window.

Likewise I can understand why people show up for work on a Monday morning but look forward to Friday to come and because it is a cycle, it does come. Behavior cycles dominate our lives daily. Communication itself is a cycle that, when understood, can yield very beneficial results or disastrous outcomes when not understood. I can tell you the outcome of the cycle that you begin by behaving in a condescending, judgmental, or accusatory manner toward someone. You will not receive a very beneficial response from the recipient of that behavior cycle at the office or at home. Even computer programs run subroutines to accomplish the program's purpose and objectives. So let's use the certainty, familiarity and momentum of cycles as a model for a systematic application in our daily quest for successful working *moment of truth* transactions.

Moment of Truth Cycle

"Normal is nothing more than a cycle on a washing machine."
Whoopi Goldberg

Think of an ordinary washing machine which is commonly used to wash clothes in everyday life. There is a round knob on the control panel that controls the washing machine cycle functions. To operate the washing machine we turn the control knob clockwise which generally cycles between the positions of wash, rinse, and spin cycles hundreds of times a year depending on our rate of usage. Now use your imagination and pretend that *you* are the washing machine control knob but instead of wash, rinse, and spin cycles, you rotate clockwise between the cycle periods of before, during, and after *moments of truth*. The Moment of Truth is that point when you come into contact with your client and was explained in detail in chapter 1 and illustrated below in fig. 8.1.

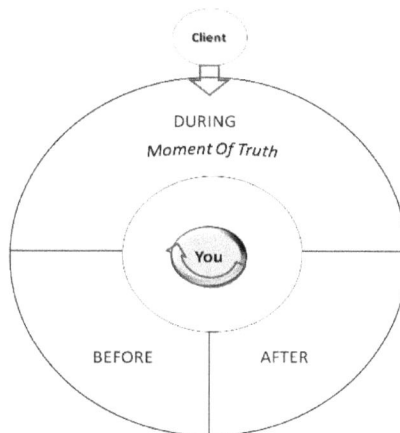

The Moment of Truth Cycles

Fig 8.1

You may transact with one, a few or many different people on any given day at any given time and all of those interchanges will be represented in the washing machine control knob model. As the model depicts, you will always be in one of the three states during the normal day except for personal hygiene in the morning at home which is an initialization time or can be viewed as a onetime *prewash cycle* in our washing machine control knob model. Otherwise it will either be *before* you encounter someone, *during* an encounter with someone, or *after* an encounter with someone or mixtures of these three normal cycles.

For instance, if you are speaking to me as one client but just finished helping another client, say on the phone, you are in both an *after* the *moment of truth* as well as a d*uring the moment of truth* state speaking to me, and may assist yet another client immediately following our conversation which currently places you in a state of b*efore* that next m*oment of truth* as well.

This entire system is centered on the *moment of truth*, how to prepare for it, what to focus on during and after it, and when to skillfully use the concepts introduced in previous chapters as tools during each of those cycle periods that will become second nature yet highly effective in your daily life. So let's put it all together.

The Before Cycle

The cycle of Preparation

We don't typically try running several miles without properly stretching and wearing the proper footwear. We don't take important exams or give reports without first studying the material. Nor does a computer just turn on and start working without running its initialization routine. Likewise we should understand that preparation is the mother of success and the small amount of time it takes to prepare ourselves to transact with others will make a huge difference in the end. The following steps make up the Before Cycle in our washing machine analogy, just as the washing machine moves through adding water, agitate, rinse and spin, so should you move through each of the following steps as you move through your own *moment of truth* Before Cycling.

Note: The service superior tools that should be focused on for the success of each cycle will be listed next to each cycle in primary and then secondary order.

For example as shown in figure 8.2:

The primary tool used for Decide and Control is **The SMART Remote Control** from chapter 4, fig4.1.

The primary tool used for Personal Maintenance is **The Performance Meter** from chapter 7, fig 7.4.

The primary tool used for Smile and Conquer is **The Behavior Display Keypad** from chapter 5, fig 5.3.

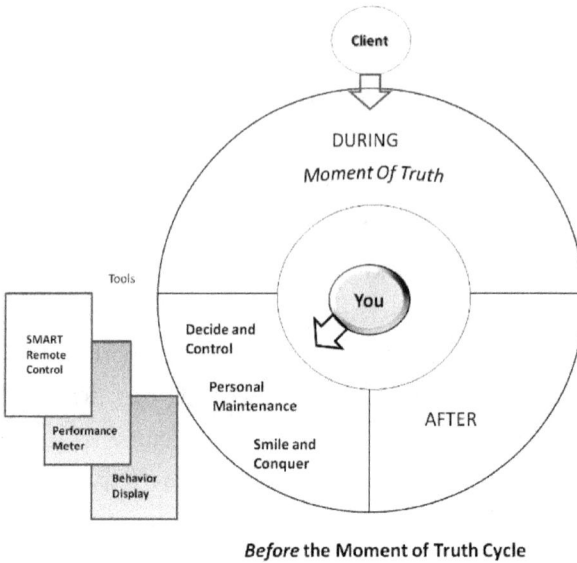

Before the Moment of Truth Cycle

Fig 8.2

Decide and Control

"Each morning when I open my eyes I say to myself: I, not events, have the power to make me happy or unhappy today. I can choose which it shall be. Yesterday is dead, tomorrow hasn't arrived yet. I have just one day, today, and I'm going to be happy in it. "
-Groucho Marx

As stated in Chapter 2, communication is a continuous process, and this is true even when you are alone. For example, right after you first wake up in the morning, you might look out the window and see that it's raining. You might say to yourself, "Oh, rain. I should get ready early because it may take longer to get to work." Or you could say to yourself, "Crap! It's going to be a lousy day." But you will place some value on the moment whether positive or negative, and your mood in the moment changes accordingly.

So when you wake up in the morning, *decide* to have a good day. Moreover, *control* your day by deciding your responses to all outside occurrences, because if you don't decide how you want your day to go, it will be decided for you. Remember your mind is like a television screen. Not making a conscious effort to control your day is like allowing your neighbor to control your television through the walls with his remote. But once you recognize that there are random thoughts in your mind that affect your mood, you can then pull out your virtual remote control and change the channel of your mind to a more positive station that will enable you to have a productive day. (Review Chapter 4 "SMART Remote Control".)

Personal Maintenance

Just as with your vehicle, working continuously without taking time out for maintenance leads to less than peak performance. If you neglect yourself it will result in less than peak performance in every aspect of your life. Since communication skills, or EI, contribute to our overall mental health, we will briefly focus on the physical side of the scale as shown in figure 8.3.

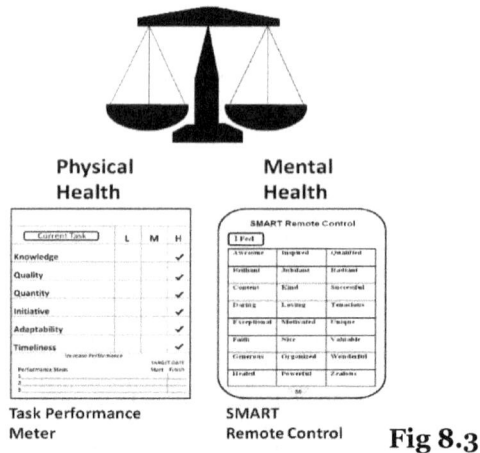

Physical Health   Mental Health

Task Performance Meter   SMART Remote Control   **Fig 8.3**

Health is About Performance

After being successful in achieving a great balance between your technical and Communication skills, leading to you being a very effective, well-rounded individual, it would be a shame to have your body give out on you while you are on your road of successfully interacting in your daily moment of truth transactions with others. Just as we don't expect our vehicles to successfully transport us to and from our various destinations without providing them the required regular maintenance and proper gas to fuel their engines, we can't expect our bodies to continue to successfully carry us from successful transaction to transaction without the required regular maintenance and proper gas to fuel our engines as well.

Three very important areas to consider are proper rest, proper diet, and proper exercise, which are the required maintenance and fuel our bodies' need to operate at peak performance. Some of the warning signs of poor personal maintenance are: difficulty focusing or falling asleep during meetings, short tempered or grouchy and feeling tired or low energy levels.

Place 1) rest, 2) diet, and 3) exercise in your task performance meter window individually and perform the OMI process on each of them after reviewing the Task Performance Meter section in chapter 7. This will prove very effective and will allow you to properly observe, measure, and increase your performance in each of these areas as projects that you will manage and rate accordingly.

Personal Hygiene

Most people already practice this but let's cover it to be on the safe side. It is unfortunate when you encounter really good people in the workplace with great skills but before you get to fully interact with them you are distracted by an unpleasant odor. And then no matter how much you like them or how good they are, that perfect moment of truth transaction is overshadowed by that annoying smell they are emitting. Shower at least once daily and use products that are strong enough for your individual needs. Powder is a good way to cut down on perspiration in addition to antiperspirants. Remember to wash clothing worn during days of heavy perspiration because the odor remains in the clothing.

The main idea is to eliminate anything that can be a hindrance to a positive Moment of Truth experience for you and the client (and to save yourself the embarrassment of being told you have an unpleasant odor, of course). It is also important that you periodically visit the restroom and straighten yourself up so that you look your best for your next Moment of Truth experience. Before leaving for work and throughout the day make sure your hair is clean and neat, and your eyes, ears, nose and mouth are clean and clear of debris. You can certainly place your personal hygiene through the Task Performance Meter OMI process to see how you fare, to ensure there are no weaknesses, or strengthen your daily regimen.

Dress for Success

Early in my career as a client support person, I realized the value of dressing for success. I started out as a computer installer responsible for setting up equipment and running cable from one workstation to another. That didn't stop me from wanting to look professional, though. I started wearing suits to work every day. People didn't treat me like just an installer; they treated me like a supervisor. The clients and my managers hated to see me on my knees connecting cables and such, and they would offer to do it themselves. My management used to hint that I should wear more casual attire, but the next day I would show up wearing another suit. It didn't take long before I was actually made a team leader because I already looked like one. It's human nature to respect professional attire. Because I always dressed like a manager, it didn't take long before I became one.

Now I'm not suggesting that everyone should go out and buy suits. However, you should have at least five matching outfits that are cleaned and pressed weekly. If you wear uniforms and your company only provides three, you should invest in two more. Make sure what you wear is clean and pressed every day. This may seem like extra work, but after it becomes a part of your daily regimen, you'll hardly notice the effort. The important thing is to look great, which will actually make you feel great and the client will feel better in your presence. Clients will actually gravitate to you because you look good! Try it yourself. The next time you are out shopping, see who you gravitate toward when you need assistance. Do you gravitate toward the casually dressed person with wrinkled clothes that are not properly fitted, or the professionally dressed person whose clothes are well fitted, pressed, and coordinated? The latter person appears more knowledgeable, competent, and confident; and you as the consumer will feel better spending your money and time with the person who appears to be the most qualified to assist you.

Smile and Conquer

It has been proven that the muscles used when smiling actually release chemicals in the body that make you healthier. That's right; you actually add time to your life when you smile. Plus it makes you look and feel better.

Smiling also disarms human beings of all titles and walks of life. Even babies react better to smiling faces. As a matter of fact, all humans react more positively to a smile than to a frown or a blank expression. Some of the documented benefits of smiling are:

- Releases endorphins, natural pain killers and serotonin into your body which is a natural feel-good drug
- Makes you look more attractive to others
- Lifts your face and makes you look and feel younger

139

- Relieves stress
- Changes your mood
- Boosts your immune system
- Projects confidence and friendliness
- Lowers blood pressure
- Is contagious!

I use a smile as a disarming tool like Clint Eastwood with his two six shooters ready to draw as he walks down the dusty street of an old western town.

As a service technician, I was frequently sent to respond to equipment service requests for someone with a very important deadline to make but must be told they will have to be inconvenienced or wait on a part to come in. Upon entering the room I greet them with the smile, and of course the smile is genuine because with the SMART Remote Control, personal maintenance and dress for success, I look, smell, and feel great! Now that they are disarmed of negativity and usually smiling themselves I can deliver the unpleasant news which would've been received a lot worse had they not engaged in the mutual preparatory smile and associated benefits. Approaching your day and subsequent moment of truth interactions without being armed with the smile and associated benefits is like sitting down to a steak dinner with a butter knife.

I suggest that you actually try your smile out in the mirror. Practice makes perfect, and the payoff is immeasurable. The first opportunity you get, put this strategy to the test: greet those who might be feeling down with a smile. You will be pleased with the results.

The During Cycle of the Moment of Truth

The During Cycle is that period when we are in contact with another person, in which you are looking for a mutually positive exchange during the overall interaction while you perform your job. And by now you realize that client service is a part of every job.

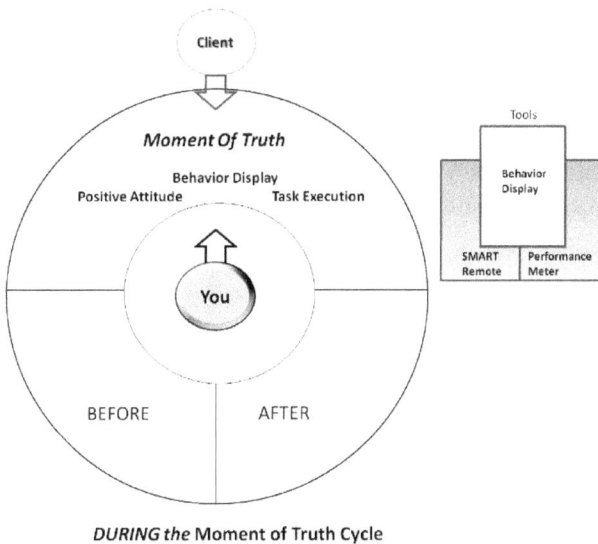

DURING the Moment of Truth Cycle

Fig 8.4

Positive Attitude

A positive attitude is an essential ingredient when dealing with the public. Positive attitude starts with a general mastery of your intra-personal communication skills discussed in chapter 3; Communication. It's the act of filtering out the available negativity present by focusing on the more positive aspects of any given situation; "the glass half full" vs. "the glass half empty" approach, in which both are true but it's a matter of what you focus on at the time. No matter how it seems, we always have a choice. Developing a predisposition to see and focus on the positive aspects is having a positive attitude and is one of the most important skills to have when dealing with people and will serve you well. Remember negativity is your enemy here.

Behavior Display

When I was young I used to hear this comedian named Flip Wilson always say *"what you see is what you get!"* Briefly visualizing your client satisfied in your mind and then working toward that goal by behaving as if that is the case is very effective. It is imperative not to dwell on undesired outcomes, but rather, only focus on the things you want to happen and over which you have direct control and don't concern yourself with things you can't control. This is your Moment of Truth, this is your stage. It's Show Time!

Occasionally, the client may have a very bad day prior to this moment, and may be ready and willing to share their negativity with everyone they meet. Don't spend too much time trying to cheer them up, but instead, concentrate on the actual step-by-step process (performance task meter chapter 7) to ensure the correctness of your tasks as the client service professional. Even in the face of total negativity on the part of a client, as a superior client service representative you will only attempt to control your portion of the Moment of Truth. This requires focusing on correctness and positive behavior flavor (behavior display chapter 5) and not allowing the negative energy that is temporarily controlling the client to control, or even affect, the unwaveringly positive image of the situation that you have established (the sun of your solar system figure 5.1).

Behavior Display Example

I was confronted with a situation like this while working as a Project Manager on a contract for a large government agency. Our organization was contracted to provide network support services for this particular agency, and a senior executive manager for this agency who was known to be a difficult person approached me while I was speaking to one of my engineers. I immediately released my engineer as soon as I recognized the level of negativity that was about to be unleashed by the client in this Moment of Truth, for I thought it best not to subject my employee to it as well. The manager first explained his reason for being so upset; a very important service that was not being done should have been done and better get done immediately. My organization was not contracted to cover this service, but the situation was still an urgent matter. I immediately focused on the correctness of the process despite the very disrespectful manner in which the client was speaking. I then let him know that it is unfortunate that this situation had arisen, but I told him, situations are made to be resolved and I'd do everything within my power to come up with a speedy resolution. This answer was unacceptable, and the client continued the verbal lashing.

I continued to show empathy toward him without accepting the negative energy and looked for possible solutions even as the client became even more agitated and began yelling. The louder he became, the more professional and pleasant I remained. His other two government employees present could not believe how calm and unaffected I was by their boss's relentless attack. Little did they know that, short of having to defend myself physically, there was no way their boss could have changed my pleasant and professional demeanor because I fully understood the power of controlling my Moment of Truth.

The client must never be given the authority to control your part in ensuring a positive exchange, and that is what happens if you shout in response to his shouting. When you are equipped with the proper tools, you give yourself that superior client service edge, and this also works at home. I had decided to have a good day before leaving home. I looked good. I smelled good. I felt good, and I continued to smile. After about five minutes of yelling, the client looked at me in disbelief. He was totally exhausted and embarrassed for losing control of his temper and displaying such nasty behavior. I, on the other hand, was totally unaffected; and the next day my company and I received a formal letter of apology from the contracting office. I was also asked if I wanted to file a formal complaint against the manager, which, of course, I declined to do. But after the incident, I received a higher level of respect from all who had witnessed it.

Because I had properly prepared myself early that morning in my Before The Moment of Truth pre-cycle, and was controlling and totally clear about the behavior I wanted displayed at that moment, this was but a small test of my superior client service skills, and my company ended up being contracted for the additional work the manager deemed so necessary, which meant increased business and increased revenue for my organization. My Behavior Display keypad proved to be the tool for me that day. I didn't even need my SMART Remote Control because my negative emotions were locked up in the basement asleep where they belonged. What an exhilarating feeling to be in control of your life, one Moment of Truth at a time.

Task Execution

No matter what the situation, *negativity* and/or *under performance* are at the core of most unsuccessful endeavors. During the Moment of Truth is when the repeated, near flawless execution of the tasks assigned to you, that your organization needs accomplished to perform its mission successfully, are displayed as discussed in chapter 7, Making the Most of Your Technical Skills. And no matter what field, industry, or position you are in, a positive outlook and a high level of performance at your job will demand successful moment of truth transactions and overall career success, period.

The After Cycle

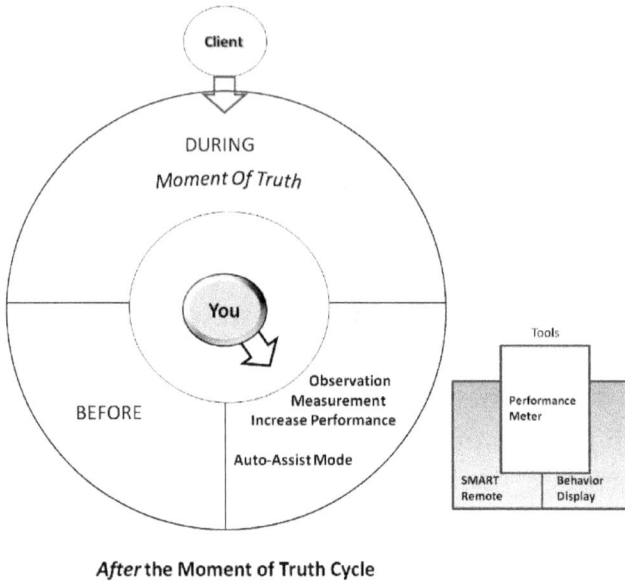

After the Moment of Truth Cycle

Fig 8.5

You will not always be in the *During* the Moment of Truth cycle, directly interacting with your client or performing your primary job or assigned duties, but at those times you could still be very effective at providing superior client service by: 1) increasing your job skills and 2) assisting others.

Observation, Measurement Increase, Performance

A very brief review of your Moment of Truth interaction or job process execution immediately following your last *During* the Moment of Truth cycle or as time permits is the goal here. By placing those

Moments of Truth transactions in your virtual Task Performance Meter observation window, covered in detail (in Chapter 7), you ensure you are at your best with your own performance management routine, keeping you focused and sharp, continually running in the background of your mind. You are then able to make small adjustments as needed to increase your performance in a certain area or improve your positive interactions with others. And being a part of a cycle, another opportunity will soon come for you to test your skills, just as the morning and weekend comes back around as a part of their cycles. Observing and measuring yourself, and increasing your performance when you are not busy is an awesome program to have running in your life.

Auto Assist Mode

In basketball, another player on your team may end up in the lane and open for a shot which is an opportunity for them to score. You can then pass the basketball to that player, which is known in that sport as an *assist*. If they score in their *Moment of Truth* experience, you get credited for the *assist*. Likewise, in the game of client service, you may find yourself in a low profile situation without a lot to do at the moment and see a client or coworker needing assistance. If you volunteer your assistance in support of their *Moment of Truth*, you help to build positive momentum to the flow of that day. Moreover, your action on someone else's behalf shows character and a higher level of understanding of the overall team mission, which is what separates superior client service representatives from the rest. Because at the end of the day everyone benefits from positive exchanges and happy clients, even in situations that don't directly affect you at the time.

As a team player, it is important to accept new challenges. In fact, in order to improve in your fulfillment of your job description and move forward on your career path, you must be faced with new challenges that will test your present level of competence and encourage your growth. Do not shy away from the new or different because these are opportunities that further your progress toward your success. In fact, as your proficiency increases in one area, allow yourself to expand into another area, even if it's "not your job". Soon this will make you an invaluable asset to any organization.

You probably don't realize that you're presented with opportunities to take your skills in new directions and to expand your proficiency in new areas every single day. These opportunities abound in the *After* the Moment of Truth Cycle.

Always look to assist someone while completing other tasks. Never hesitate to ask someone: May I Help You? This is called by most, "going the extra mile," and that extra mile is more important than you ever dreamed – both to the success of the enterprise that employs you, and to your journey along your career path.

When you are asked to perform tasks that you feel are outside of your job description, ask yourself would gaining a proficiency in that skill benefit me in any way or at any time in my future? The *After* Cycle is the perfect time to grow skills for future positions, free on the job training (OJT).

And since some of us learn more about ourselves as we go and are not sure exactly what field we will end up in, taking advantage of many opportunities within our path may prove advantageous.

One day my daughter emailed me from work saying she wanted my opinion about something later after work. That evening she expressed concern that her manager had placed her in charge of managing the office leave calendar and other similar, management-type tasking. This entailed having to deal with her peers as if she were their manager at times, so basically more responsibility without an additional title or salary increase. I then shared the *After* Cycle perspective and she decided to take on the additional responsibility and recorded the additional tasks in her job description to be mentioned at her next review.

Three months later, she was promoted to Office Manager with a nice bump in salary. She didn't see herself as management material back then but it is very apparent now as she has exceeded expectations in that role. This evolution happened during my daughter's regular *Moment of Truth* cycling but the additional skills needed for the non current job description tasks had to be developed in her *After the Moment of Truth* cycle.

That completes the entire Moment of Truth Cycle, circle back around to the *Before the Moment of Truth* cycle and blaze trails.

Chapter Nine

The Next Level

If there is one thing I am certain of it's that evolution like the arrow of time is always moving forward. Mankind will always continue to make strides in science and technology, discovering new and better ways to enhance the quality of our lives. This book has introduced a set of tools that are to be used by you as mental focusing devices to enhance the quality of your life at work and at home. They are designed to create a pathway through the many situational distractions that constantly bombard us, and to help us to maintain a positive, forward-moving course of personal and professional accomplishment with noticeable results. I have noticed a laxness caused by years of viewing entertainment screens which are devices that can only display two dimensions, but attempt to depict a world of three dimensions. And even though we don't all agree how many total dimensions of reality there are, we all agree there are at least three. So I believe our minds have gotten a little lazy not having to utilize our imaginations much. Television consistently just hands us the imagery as our mental diet, and in a sense we've stopped searching for additional levels of consciousness or at the very least feel uncomfortable when asked to think a little outside the box and flex our imaginary mental muscles.

A physical remote control can sit on a stand forever and never be of any use unless someone eventually picks it up, turns it on and points it to operate the screen. Likewise, the tools provided in this system are designed to be activated by your focused attention. They are to be aimed at real situations through your imagination and your ability to see beyond the two dimensional realities we've been feeding on, to focus and control your feelings, behavior, and performance in a new way. All that is needed is for you to power them with your imagination, and after a short period of time you will perform those tasks automatically without the need to carry the cards because of the amazing minds and hearts we all possess. This book is asking you to believe that we are connected by a force you cannot see that exchanges energy vital to us all, and to develop yourself positively because you have an impact on the overall whole of humanity.

The book asks you to believe that through intra-personal communication between your brain and heart your feelings will respond like tiny soldiers awaiting your every command. You are being asked to take conventional systems like behavioral science, psychology, performance management, quality management, and process improvement and condense them into quick mental exercises which may relinquish the need for extensive training and much oversight to recreate yourself and increase your performance. However, it is not an attempt to replace those fields of study. We are simply borrowing the attributes that are effective for our Superior Client Service model. Without question our minds and hearts are the most sophisticated phenomenon mankind has ever encountered. Understanding the process of Emotions-Behavior-Performance and mastering the areas these tools represent is an undertaking with enormous rewards at work, at home and everywhere else! To do so is to be a Service Superior!

I look forward to servicing you in *the Moment!*

Appendix A

Scale Focus Points

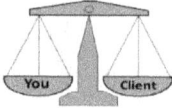

Focus on Vendor/Client exchange balance during the *moment of truth*. (Chapter 1)

Technical Skills   Communication Skills
Left Brain   Right Brain

Focus on a balance of proficiency with your Technical skills and your Communication skills. (Chapter 3)

Physical Health   Mental Health

Task Performance Meter   SMART Remote Control

Focus on your Mental and Physical health Balance and the tools to utilize for each. (Chapter 8)

Technical Skills   Communication Skills

Task Performance Meter   SMART Remote Control

Focus on the tools to utilize for optimum Technical and Communication skill balance. (Chapter 8)

The Major Solution
Service Superior Toolkit

These mental tools are in the form of Smart cards that fit in the palm of your hand that can be carried around during the day and are available at www.servicesuperior.com.

About The Author

Major Lewis has demonstrated a passion for connecting with people and championing their mental, physical and spiritual wellbeing throughout his career. At age 23 he was President and Chairman of the Army Community Service (ACS) European Division volunteer initiative, a comprehensive social service program that identified emerging social problems and assisted the community of military personnel, retirees, civilians and families located in the Northern Germany area. Major also founded and chaired the Bremerhaven Community Church Brotherhood Ministries and Community Outreach Programs located in Bremerhaven Germany that provided food, shelter, and activities for the local and international population of that region.

In the United States, Major served in the U.S ARMY 82nd Airborne division where he brought his unique perspective and positive energy that influenced those he served under as well as the troops under his command. After the military Major held several mid to senior-level client service management positions (CEO, Director, Program Manager, and Project Manager) and teamed with many government-contracted Information Technology (IT) and Communications firms.

With a proven track record of outstanding communication, managerial, and client service techniques, Major founded The Major Solution LLC that delivered on-site IT Client Enterprise Management Support, process improvement, and client service training for government contractors providing support for federal, local, and state government offices. Major's underlining principles and commitment to the superior client service philosophy, allowed the companies he represented to enjoy favorable performance ratings, extended contracts, and government-issued acknowledgements and awards.

Major continually gives back to the community by giving freely of his time and service to empower disadvantaged, at-risk youth. Major encourages them to escape negativity by cultivating positive and healthy lifestyles through the tools that develop self esteem, focus, and professionalism.

Major provides consulting services, coaching and training for selected businesses, associations, non-profit organizations, and individuals nationwide. Requests for information about these services, as well as inquiries about availability for speeches and seminars, should be directed to info@themajorsolution.com. Or visit our website at www.servicesuperior.com.

www.ingramcontent.com/pod-product-compliance
Lightning Source LLC
LaVergne TN
LVHW051237080426
835513LV00016B/1643